THE COMPLETE BOOK OF
HUMMINGBIRDS

THE COMPLETE BOOK OF
HUMMINGBIRDS

TONY TILFORD

Thunder Bay
P·R·E·S·S

San Diego, California

Thunder Bay Press

An imprint of the Baker & Taylor Publishing Group

10350 Barnes Canyon Road, San Diego, CA 92121

www.thunderbaybooks.com

Produced by Salamander Books,
an imprint of Anova Books Company Ltd.,
10 Southcombe Street, London W14 0RA, U.K.

All notations of errors or omissions should be addressed to Thunder Bay Press, Editorial Department, at the above address. All other correspondence (author inquiries, permissions) concerning the content of this book should be addressed to Salamander Books, 10 Southcombe Street, London W14 0RA, U.K.

Library of Congress Cataloging-in-Publication Data

Tilford, Tony.
  The complete book of hummingbirds / Tony Tilford.
      p. cm.
  Includes bibliographical references.
  ISBN-13: 978-1-59223-967-2
  ISBN-10: 1-59223-967-6
  1. Hummingbirds. I. Title.
  QL696.A558T55 2008
  598.7'64--dc22

                                  2008017172

Printed and bound by Times Printing, Malaysia.

2 3 4 5 12 11 10 09

Page 2: Rufous Hummingbird (*Selasphorus rufus*)

Contents

Introduction

Jewels in Flight

Although this simple title has been used by others, I cannot find a better description, and it seems neither can those who have bestowed the common names on a large proportion of the hummingbirds. Emerald, sapphire, ruby, azure, garnet, amethyst, tourmaline, and topaz are just a few jewels; all these names of brightly colored, precious gems have also been used to describe the beautiful colors of hummingbirds. Reading through the "Checklist of Hummingbirds" at the back of this book, one can be easily forgiven for mistaking it as a catalog of gemstones and precious metals.

But it goes further than that, as many evocative names, such as woodnymph, scintillant, brilliant, and mountain-gem, are also used. Other names, such as coquette, streamertail, puffleg, plumeleteer, visorbearer, and spatuletail, seem more reminiscent of a carnival. Of course, there are many hummingbirds with more descriptive names, such as awlbill, sabrewing, plovercrest, coronet, firecrown, and thornbill—and then there are those that describe their origin, such as Carib, Inca, and Hillstar. Even the more subdued brown, red, and grayish group identified as

6

the Hermits have a name that describes not only their often reclusive nature but also the duller coloration associated with a being living in solitude. The scientific names are similarly inclined to be beautifully descriptive, but that is to be expected for such a fascinating and lovely family of birds.

Left: The male Long-tailed Sylph (*Aglaiocercus kingi*) is one of the most easily recognized hummingbirds.

Opposite: The Velvet-Purple Coronet (*Boissonneaua jardini*) illustrates the effects of light; from behind, it is dark, almost black, while its breast is a glittering blue.

9

Hummingbirds and Humans

The family name of "hummingbird" was obviously derived from the sound caused by the very fast beating of their wings. With the fastest beat of any bird, approaching 200 beats per second, hummingbirds' wings move so rapidly that they cannot be seen by the human eye, but the low-pitched hum is audible to those close enough to hear.

Humans have forever been fascinated by hummingbirds and have generally treated them with respect. They pose no threat to our livelihood and are elements of beauty, giving pleasure wherever they are seen. However, they have been persecuted in the past. Historically, and even to the present, native peoples of South America used them as embellishments for their dress. Iridescent feathers and, often, whole skins were used by the Aztecs and Mayans to adorn their ceremonial dress. The Incas and Nazcas of the Andes also held the hummingbird in very high esteem, and the huge figures carved into the desert plateaus of Peru are thought to be depictions of hummingbirds. In Victorian times, hummingbirds were collected for the taxidermy trade and huge collections set up under glass domes can still be seen in many museums around the world. Toward the end of the nineteenth century, millions of hummingbird skins were imported into Europe for the millinery and fashion trade. The beauty of the plumage on these garments has now all but disappeared.

There is still a small trade in live hummingbirds for bird enthusiasts, but most species are now well protected. The trade is strictly regulated by the Washington Convention on International Trade in Endangered Species (CITES) due to the continued concern for the status of most of the species. All hummingbirds are covered by these international laws, and most countries strictly adhere to them. Fortunately, many of the birds now exported are going to very dedicated birders who are at last

Below: These illustrations of Cayenne Fairies (*Trochilus auritus*) are from John Gould's *A Monograph of the Trochilidae, or Family of Hummingbirds* (1849–1861). Gould's collection of stuffed hummingbirds fascinated visitors to London's 1851 Great Exhibition.

10

gaining the knowledge and experience to breed them in captivity. Captive breeding success has been poor in the past, but given the right conditions and species knowledge, as well as the availability of specially formulated foods, there is no reason that greater success should not be achieved in the future. The benefit of keeping these lovely creatures in captivity is that successful breeding may eventually be a useful conservation tool in saving endangered species.

Above: Handling hummingbirds, such as this juvenile Calliope Hummingbird (*Stellula calliope*), requires an extremely delicate and skilled touch. A special license is needed to study these protected birds.

Currently, the most threatened species of hummingbird is thought to be the Hook-billed Hermit (*Glaucis dohrnii*) from eastern Brazil. Only about fifty are estimated to be alive today, but as the population is drastically fragmented and difficult to count, there could be more. They are a lowland forest-dwelling species, and their habitat is under enormous pressure from human intrusion and destruction. With the huge expansion of towns, roads, industry, agriculture, logging, and mining, conservation measures stand little chance against human onslaught.

Left: This decorated Nazca vase (circa 100–800) shows hummingbirds around a flower.

Opposite: These ancient lines on the desert plateau in Peru are thought to depict a hummingbird.

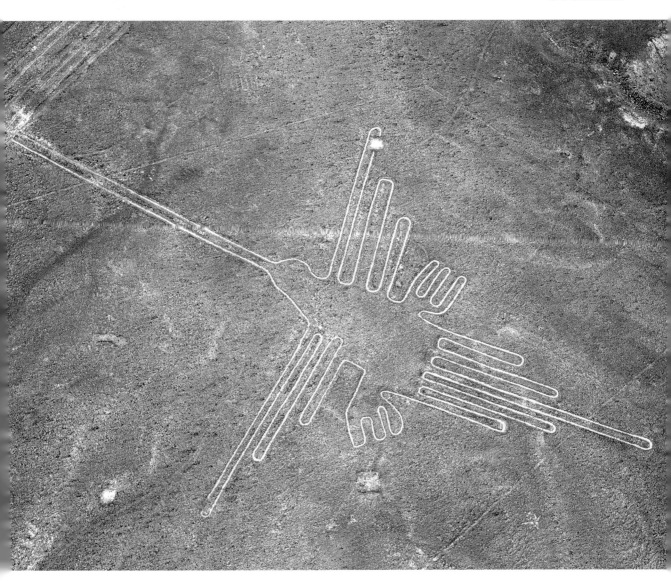

Other highly endangered species include the Honduran Emerald (*Polyerata luciae*), Juan Fernandez Firecrown (*Sephanoides fernandensis*), Scissor-tailed Hummingbird (*Hylonympha macrocerca*), Sapphire-bellied Hummingbird (*Lepidopyga lilliae*), and the Black-breasted Puffleg (*Eriocnemis nigrivestis*). As would be expected, the main threat to all of these rare species is humankind's slow but persistent destruction of their habitat. The Turquoise-throated Puffleg (*Eriocnemis godini*), an endemic species from northern Ecuador, is currently known only from museum specimens and is thought to be extinct, as its forest habitat has been completely destroyed.

Evolution

Hummingbirds are thought to be closely related to the swifts (*Apodidae*) and treeswifts (*Hemiprocnidae*); more because of their anatomical and morphological similarities. It is unknown whether they have common ancestry or whether the two avian forms have become similar, but it may not be coincidence that the two share some unique elements of body chemistry. Perhaps they were alike at one time, and a divergence of form commenced many millions of years ago. There are theories that this may have occurred when the tectonic plate on which South America presently stands broke away from Gondwanaland (the ancient supercontinent), but only in time may science discover the true relationships.

Biology

The likeness of the swifts and hummingbirds is based on the similarities of neck musculature and the way nerves are supplied to the wing muscles,

Below: The Ruby-throated Hummingbird (*Archilochus colubris*) can fly at speeds of up to fifty miles per hour. Its wings beat between forty and eighty times per second.

as well as the more familiar comparison of the skeleton associated with flight.

Hummingbirds stand apart in their adaptation to hovering flight, which appears well designed to exploit nectar from flowering plants. The skeleton has adapted in unique ways to allow the wings to move differently from other avian forms. Hummingbirds depend entirely on powerful flight muscles and the suitable skeleton to which they are attached. In addition to a proportionally longer and deeper sternum, they also have eight pairs of ribs, compared to the six of most other bird families. To allow flexibility of the wing as it moves almost 180 degrees, the sternum has a shallow depression at its junction with the powerful coracoid bones. This acts as a socket for the ball-shaped end of the short wing bone (humerus), much like a conventional mechanical

Above: Hummingbirds are capable of rapid straight flight, as can be seen by this Rufous Hummingbird (*Selasphorus rufus*).

ball-and-socket joint. The wing bones, equivalent to the humerus, radius, and ulna of the human arm, are much shorter than those adapted for conventional avian flight, and they terminate at another series of bones that support the ten main flight feathers. These bones, comparative to the bones of the hand, are proportionally much longer. Unlike other small birds, hummingbirds have only six or seven secondary wing feathers instead of the customary nine. In general, the ten primary flight feathers decrease in size from the long outer feathers inward toward the secondary feathers; however, a few species deviate from this rule.

The combination of these mechanical factors has resulted in a very adaptable flight machine that can be compared to a helicopter. Hummingbirds have the ability not only to hover but also to fly forward, backward, and occasionally even upside down.

The advantages of this mechanical design allow lift to be achieved on both forward and return wing strokes of the figure-eight pattern of movement undertaken during hovering flight. On the forward stroke, the pressure of air causing lift is on the bottom surface of the wing feathers, but as they rotate through ninety degrees for the return, the pressure changes to what is normally the top surface but is now facing down, once again generating lift. Therefore, the bird can hold its position in the air with just a balancing control from the tail.

So much emphasis is put on the hovering ability of hummingbirds that normal forward flight is frequently forgotten. They are remarkably good at flying and, indeed, for the long-distance migrations performed by some species, it is absolutely essential. However, like helicopters, most do not have the endurance that more conventional flying machines do. They need to refuel more frequently, so long distances are often covered in a series of short journeys. The exceptions to this pattern are those few North American migrants that accumulate deposits of fat to enable them to cover long distances without stopping to feed.

A hummingbird's routine flight pattern seems to consist mainly of bouts of hovering flight at feeding stations interspersed with fairly fast, straight forward dashes in between. Scientific study of hummingbirds in wind tunnels has established flying speeds of between thirty and fifty miles per hour, but in the wild, some species are known to get up to sixty miles per hour. In bouts of chasing, it is estimated that speeds approaching a hundred miles per hour can be achieved.

The muscle mass responsible for this specialized flight adaptation accounts for 30 percent of the total body mass, approximately 50 percent more than for any other strong-flying bird. These muscles demand large volumes of oxygen, especially when hovering, and consequently the heart is also proportionately larger. The heart normally beats at 500 to 600 times a minute, but can achieve almost 1,000 beats per minute when exceptionally fast responses are required.

The close association of hummingbirds with swifts has been linked in part to their likeness in neck musculature. It is thought that the special arrangement of the bird's neck allows fast responses of head movement, particularly from side to side, enabling them to catch aerial insects while in high-speed flight.

Above: White-tailed Emerald (*Elvira chionura*). Unlike most other birds, hummingbirds can hover for prolonged periods.

Plumage

As with most other species, plumage coloration is closely associated with behavior. Some birds need to display their characteristics, whereas others need to hide them.

Quite obviously, breeding females and immature birds need to remain more concealed, as they are particularly vulnerable to predators. Males, on the other hand, generally need to stand out, particularly if they are polygamous, as is the case with hummingbirds. Not only do males use their plumage to attract partners, but they also use it for territorial

Below: Flame-throated Sunangel (*Heliangelus micraste*).The gorget feathers of male hummingbirds are often highly iridescent.

Above: The vividly colored Rainbow Starfrontlet (*Coeligena iris*) from Ecuador exemplifies its name.

defense, posturing against other males regardless of species. The difference in plumage between the sexes is more pronounced in species of more open habitats; for those that inhabit more closed and frequently darker environments such as forests, the iridescence of the males is sometimes absent altogether.

The feathers of adult hummingbirds are most interesting because they lack the downy underlay present in other species, and there are considerably fewer of them. Although a few downy feathers are present while the chick is in the nest, those are shed soon after fledging. This is thought to be an adaptation that has become necessary to dissipate the large amount of heat generated within the body by the hummingbird's vigorous flight activity.

The iridescence of hummingbird feathers, particularly those on the gorgets (throat feathers) and crest plumage of the males, is caused by the physical structure of the feathers. Feather barbules (small barbs fringing the feather) contain layers of minute platelets (very thin melanin structures containing air sacs), each acting as a light interference medium, refracting light waves to produce different-colored lighting effects. Within the platelets, the melanin is often pigmented, which also has an effect on the colors produced. Depending on the angle of light reflecting from the feather, it may vary considerably from being intensely brilliant to having no iridescence at all.

As for most other birds, the pigmented color of the primary and secondary wing feathers gives hummingbirds their generally dull appearance. In fact, most hummingbirds' wings are a very similar color of dark brown to black, with infrequent tinged variations.

19

Opposite: The Violet-bellied Hummingbird (*Damophila julie*) is found in Colombia, Ecuador, Panama, and Peru.

Below: The brilliant red throat feathers of the male Ruby-throated Hummingbird (*Archilochus colubris*) are unmistakable.

Only very occasionally, such as in the Purple-throated Carib (*Eulampis jugularis*), do the feathers have an iridescent sheen, and in some species the wing coverts are brightly iridescent. These characteristics are undoubtedly due to the feather structure and the need for a strong and durable flight membrane. The flight feathers have small, hooked barbules so that they can attach to their adjacent member and provide a cohesive membrane. Generally, the small, highly reflective platelets are no advantage in this type of structure and are usually missing; as a result, the wings have a dull appearance.

The tails of hummingbirds vary considerably in shape and size from the short, straight cut of many species to the long, elaborate extensions of species such as the Marvelous Spatuletail (*Loddigesia mirabilis*). However, almost all have ten tail feathers—except the Marvelous Spatuletail, which has four. With so many variations in shape and size, the differences are thought to have occurred through the birds' adaptation to situations of habitat and behavior.

Feeding

Opposite: A female Rufous
Hummingbird (*Selasphorus
rufus*) feeds from a pink
monkeyflower.

Hummingbirds invariably feed on nectar, and are most often seen hovering at the flowers from which they extract nectar along with a little pollen.

Nectar is a necessary food source, providing the essential and easily convertible energy demanded by their mode of flight. To maintain their energy requirements, hummingbirds drink several times their body weight in nectar each day and in the process may visit up to a thousand flowers. Their long, hollow, and extensible tongues are forked at the tip, each half of the split tip being channel-shaped. Nectar is taken from the flowers into these channels by capillary action but is also assisted by a rapid licking motion. The bill serves not only as a guide for the long tongue but also as a mechanism for squeezing the nectar back into the digestive system. Regular feeding at around ten-minute intervals is essential for most species to maintain their energy requirements. In between feedings, the birds go into a state of torpor to allow the food time to digest. Besides the familiar hovering flight used by hummingbirds to get access to flowers, many also get to their food plant by perching on nearby plants or even hanging from them while maintaining their balance by beating their wings in partial flight.

Below: A female Violet-bellied
Hummingbird (*Damophila
julie*). Hummingbirds are
attracted to bright red, tubular
flowers.

For most species, insects and spiders make up as much as 10 percent of the hummingbird's food intake, providing much of the bird's essential protein requirements. Several methods are used to catch insects, but in individuals, the system used is generally determined by the bird's bill shape. Species with long bills are more suited to gleaning insects and spiders from foliage while hovering, whereas short-billed species are better adapted to hawking flies and wasps. Species in between often use both methods.

The bird's bill shape also plays an important role in the efficiency with which

nectar can be extracted from flowers. The great variation in shape among hummingbirds' bills determines which flowers they can exploit. For instance, long, tubular flowers require a long and often decurved bill for access, whereas short-billed species are more suited to shallower blooms unless they are able to pierce the base of the flower or use holes already pierced by species such as the Bananaquit *(Coereba flaveola)* or flowerpeckers.

At times of food shortage, such as during migration and when flowers are scarce, hummingbirds will resort to other food sources. The sweet sap oozing from trees damaged by woodpeckers, in particular the Sapsuckers *(Sphyrapicus spp.)*, is frequently exploited by hummingbirds migrating to North America when they arrive early to their breeding grounds. This

Below: This male Ruby-throated Hummingbird (*Archilochus colubris*) shows its long, extensible tongue.

attraction is a valuable source of nourishment, not only for its sugary content but also because it attracts many insects on which the birds can feed. Similarly, hummingbirds are known to consume the sugary excretions deposited by insects.

Whereas many of the smaller species tend to have feeding territories confined to a relatively small group of abundantly flowering shrubs or trees, others depend on "trap-lining," the process of visiting widely distributed suitable flowers in a regular and often set pattern. There are others that behave more generally and adopt both procedures, but because of their intermediate size are able to ignore the threats of the more territorial birds.

Above: A female Ruby-throated Hummingbird (*Archilochus colubris*) excretes surplus fluid.

The energy required to support a hummingbird's high level of activity is proportionally immense, and it is understandable that this group of birds has the highest metabolic rate per unit of body weight in the avian world. Their digestive system must ensure rapid conversion of food into energy, so its specialized adaptation allows nectar to pass directly from the crop into the small intestine, bypassing the stomach altogether. Within a short time span of about fifteen minutes, it is completely digested. On the other hand, solid food passes from the crop into the first section of the stomach, where protein is digested by acids and enzymes. From there, it continues to be digested in the second, smaller part of the stomach before being passed into the small intestine.

It is estimated that hummingbirds consume more than one and a half times their body weight in fluids and nectar each day, of which much is excreted as urine. This can often be observed at feeders as fluid is passed in a jet from the bird's vent. Could this be another reason these birds have also been known as "rainbirds"?

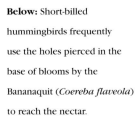

Below: Short-billed hummingbirds frequently use the holes pierced in the base of blooms by the Bananaquit (*Coereba flaveola*) to reach the nectar.

27

Energy needs demand that hummingbirds have a regular intake of nectar when they are active, which even extends into dusk and before dawn. Fortunately, many have good night vision and are not wholly diurnal as would be expected. This is especially so with some of the high-altitude species, which may have extra demands on their metabolism in colder climes.

Above: The Sword-billed Hummingbird (*Ensifera ensifera*) is well adapted to take nectar from long, bell-shaped flowers.

Artificial Feeding and Gardening for Hummingbirds

It is normal for only part of the hummingbird's essential diet to be provided by artificial feeding—a replacement for the nectar usually obtained from flowers. Hummingbirds can be attracted to artificial feeding stations, but they must also be able to forage for insects and flies. They will come to feeders and accept the easily obtained man-made nectar replacements, but will naturally wander around seeking the essential protein provided by insect food. Birds kept in captivity either because they are sick or

injured or for conservation and study must always be provided with ample amounts of live food in the form of fruit flies and the like, in addition to nectar replacements.

Above: A Glowing Puffleg (*Eriocnemis vestitus*) at a garden feeder.

Attracting wild hummingbirds to feeders is an extremely enjoyable pastime, and certainly boosts the population where natural nectar is in short supply. In many parts of the United States, the population of hummingbirds is far above the level at which natural nectar supplies would support. These "hummingbird hot spots" are usually around feeding stations set up specially to study the birds, and they give enormous enjoyment to those present in the vicinity.

There are numerous proprietary feeders on the market, as well as ready-made nectar mixes that need the addition of boiling water. Most of the mixes are simply sugar with a little coloring and an additive to prevent fermentation. The coloring has no advantage whatsoever, as it is the strength of the nectar alone that attracts the birds. If the nectar is too weak or too strong, the birds may prefer to forage elsewhere. It is much cheaper to prepare simple sugar and water solutions and replace them regularly, throwing away any leftovers. What is important is that hummingbirds must never be fed honey or artificial sweeteners and any food offered must never be allowed to go stale. In hot weather, sugar mixtures deteriorate rapidly and may need to be changed daily. Ants,

Opposite: A juvenile Rufous Hummingbird (*Selasphorus rufus*) takes advantage of a well-placed artificial feeder.

28

Above: A female Rufous Hummingbird (*Selasphorus rufus*) feeds from a 'Sani Pass' Sensation (*Phygelius aequalis*).

wasps and other insects can also be a problem when they find the easily obtained food, for they discourage the hummingbirds and can also trigger early fermentation of the "nectar." They are, however, not easy to deter other than by using feeders with special bee guards or, in the case of ants, rubbing the support wires with a sticky substance such as salad oil or by moving the feeder. Fermenting substances only encourage fungal growths, which are harmful to the birds' health, so fresh food in clean containers is a must. It should be changed every two or three days.

To prepare your own hummingbird food, a mixture of one part sugar to four parts drinking water should be heated and allowed to simmer for a couple of minutes to kill off any bacteria and reduce harmful chemicals. When it has cooled, store any unused food in a clean container in the refrigerator. Prepare only enough for a few days at a time, and thoroughly clean all containers every two or three days.

Positioning feeders around the yard or in a location near the house where they can easily be observed will invariably attract hummingbirds,

29

but in general, they prefer the natural nectar from flowers. The best bet to encourage hummingbirds close to your home is to adopt both methods by also planting suitable hardy herbs and shrubs that will give a succession of flowers throughout the year. Trumpet-shaped blooms, particularly red, orange, and yellow, are like magnets to hummingbirds.

Trees, shrubs, and perennial plants are the least trouble when established, and there are many to choose from. Even trees that are not regularly used by hummingbirds can be made useful by allowing vines such as honeysuckle, morning glory, and trumpet creeper to climb up them. Azaleas and mimosa may take time before they flower and can grow to a reasonable size, and the perennial lilies, phlox, and hibiscus are not difficult to spread around the garden.

Above: Most hummingbirds, including these Andean Emeralds (*Amazilia franciae*), are attracted to bright red trumpet-shaped blooms.

A little more effort is needed with the annual bedding plants. They not only produce a very colorful garden in their own right but can also be extremely attractive to hummingbirds throughout the summer months. Plants to try include begonia, foxglove, geranium, gladiolas, hollyhock, impatiens, Indian paintbrush, lantana, nasturtium, nicotinia, petunia, red salvia, shrimp plant, spider plant, sweet William, and Texas olive.

As a word of warning, hummingbirds are very sensitive to pesticides and herbicides, so the use of chemical sprays is to be avoided.

Below: The Violet-crowned Woodnymph (*Thalurania colombica*) is extremely defensive of flowers in its feeding territory.

31

Hummingbirds' Symbiosis with Flowering Plants

The symbiotic relationship between hummingbirds and plants has resulted in a wide variety of adaptations between the two on which both are, as a family, mutually dependent, or at least partly so. However, there is little evidence of specific interdependence. Competition for nectar exists with bees as well as other insects, and to some extent they must all play a part in pollination.

Many hummingbirds search out large, bell-shaped pendant flowers that are brightly colored, usually red, orange, or yellow and often with white inner petals or corollas. Others are attracted to white flowers with red markings, such as those found on some of the epiphytes. During the process of extracting nectar, plant pollination is achieved as the

Below: This Emerald-bellied Woodnymph (*Thalurania fannyi hypochlora*) competes with bees at an artificial feeder.

hummingbird transfers pollen from one flower to another. Interestingly, hummingbird-pollinated flowers are seldom scented and only infrequently attract insects. The color stimulus provided by these plants is heavily weighted toward the red end of the spectrum, the long wavelengths to which hummingbird vision is most sensitive. Hummingbirds associate these colors in flowers with food availability, in particular the energy content of the nectar.

Within many of the flowers visited by hummingbirds reside tiny mites, which also feed on nectar and pollen. As the bird is feeding, mites move onto its bill and into the nasal cavity, where they are transported, unbeknown and harmless to the hummingbird, to a new host plant, where they will begin another breeding cycle.

Above: Hummingbird flower mites are visible on the bill of this Fawn-breasted Brilliant (*Heliodoxa rubinoides*). Hummingbirds transport mites from one flower to another as they sip nectar.

Opposite: Female Rufous Hummingbirds (*Selasphorus rufous*) reluctantly share a feeder. Hummingbirds can be aggressively competitive over feeding territory.

Below: This juvenile Ruby-throated Hummingbird (*Archilochus colubris*) takes advantage of rainfall to clean its plumage.

Behavior

The behavior of hummingbirds is, for the most part, governed by their environment and habits. Their adaptations as nectar-feeding species require that they move around according to their specialized needs and reliance on nectar-bearing food sources. Consequently, their feeding habits are solitary occupations and males and females lead completely separate lives, and even become very aggressive with each other and with other nectar-feeding species. They seek out those flowers that are especially rich in energy, and inevitably there will be great competition around good food sources. Individuals set up territories around such flowering plants and vigorously defend them against intruders. Their aggression can be extreme to the point of attacking anything, even humans, that they see as a potential rival for the food supply.

Leading such solitary lives is in keeping with their polygamous breeding behavior; the very brief acts of copulation are often the only time the sexes come into contact. At the start of the breeding season, the males of several hummingbird species arrive on the breeding grounds prior to the females and group together in bands, or leks, around potentially rich food sources to vie for females as they pass by.

Hummingbirds really seem to enjoy bathing and do so several times a day, often followed by vigorous shaking and long bouts of preening. Some will hover above shallow pools, suddenly dropping in and often completely submerging. Others find puddles, either on the ground or in large leaves, in which to land and then soak themselves by splashing their wings. During

rainfall, they often sit out in the open with outstretched wings and a well-spread tail, just catching the raindrops on their plumage. Waterfalls and water sprinklers in parks and gardens are other favorite places to bathe and catch falling water drops.

Such behavior is all a necessary part of their feather care—the birds attempt to maintain their plumage in an efficient and clean condition, as they must undoubtedly become soiled with nectar and pollen during their feeding activities. After bathing, preening plays an important part in the oiling of feathers, ensuring that they stay waterproof in often rainy and humid conditions.

36

Above: Booted Racquet-tails (*Ocreatus underwoodii*) display their plumage.

Left: Buff-tailed Coronets (*Boissonneaua flavescens*). Like other birds, hummingbirds communicate through sound and visual display.

Opposite: Copper-rumped Hummingbirds (*Amazilia tobaci*) fight for territory.

before they fledge. At birth, two rows of short, bristly down feathers develop along the back, and the eyes are unopened. A feeding stimulus is given to the chick by the mother, who touches the head or back feathers with her bill.

Only in the second week of life do the youngsters open their eyes, and at this time, the body feathers also really begin to show. Close to fledging, the mother will hover over the nest, creating a downdraft, which visibly disturbs the chicks' plumage, and they start to gape for food.

Once the chicks are out of the nest, the mother continues to feed her young for another three weeks or so, but they usually remain in the close vicinity of the nest during this period, often hidden in the tree canopy. The young are gradually persuaded by the mother's persistent calls to follow her to convenient flowering plants, where they will soon learn to feed for themselves.

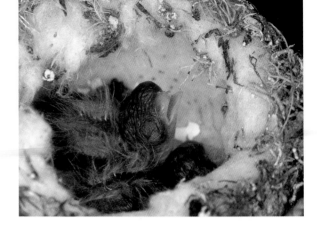

Above: This nest is lined with soft plant down and disguised with small pieces of locally collected plant debris.

Left: An Anna's Hummingbird (*Calypte anna*) on a lichen-decorated nest.

Opposite: An Anna's Hummingbird (*Calypte anna*) feeds her chick.

Distribution, Migration, and Movements

The family of hummingbirds, the Trochilidae, are found in the neotropical regions of the New World in an area covering all of South America and its adjacent islands, northward through the Caribbean and North America as far as Nova Scotia in the east and Alaska in the west. The most northerly breeding hummingbird is the Rufous Hummingbird (*Selasphorus rufus*), which is found in Alaska, and the most southerly is the Green-backed Firecrown (*Sephanoides sephanoides*), which breeds in Tierra del Fuego. There are now thought to be 328 species of New World hummingbirds, of which Costa Rica alone has fifty-one. The highest density of hummingbird

Below: Less than three inches in length, the Calliope Hummingbird (*Stellula calliope*) is the smallest long-distance migrant.

42

species is found through Colombia, Ecuador, and northern Peru, where around 150 species have been observed.

Long-distance seasonal migration of hummingbirds is limited to only a small proportion of the species: those that have their breeding grounds in the United States and Canada north of the tropics, and those in southern South America. However, many disperse after breeding to exploit better food resources or for more suitable climatic conditions.

In reality, the study of hummingbird movements has only just begun. Large-scale banding of hummingbirds is both difficult and not very remunerative record-wise due not only to the size of the birds but also to the chances of getting adequate returns from nonpopulated areas and regions with difficult terrain.

Most of the knowledge of hummingbird movement today is concentrated around only a few species and relies on the fact that at certain times of the year birds are present or absent in a given region. It is generally surmised that birds are traveling between regions. This perception goes a little further in speculating that in some species the sexes arrive and leave at different times, but there is very little known about how this correlates to the bird's age. Within the vast area of known hummingbird habitats in North America, where banding and study may be comparatively easy, much of the work is done at well-established feeding stations. It is when the birds leave these stations that the problem becomes particularly difficult. Studies in this region have shown that most North American species of hummingbirds are only partial migrants. That is, there is a tendency for birds at the northern boundaries of the range to move to more favorable climates for the winter, whereas those in acceptable conditions remain sedentary. Four North American species— the Calliope, Rufous, Black-chinned, and Ruby-throated hummingbirds— are exceptions in that they all migrate outside their breeding range for the winter. It is known that the long-distance journeys performed by these species, especially the Ruby-throated Hummingbird, are often nonstop and even involve flying approximately 500 miles over the Gulf of Mexico. It is much more likely that many take the easier but longer coastal route around the gulf. Whichever route is taken, it is an incredible feat, especially for the Calliope Hummingbird, the world's smallest long-distance migrant.

As with other species of long-distance migratory birds, hummingbirds need to put on body fat if they are to undertake long journeys without

43

feeding. Increases in body weight prior to venturing on long migrations can be as much as 60 percent for the Broad-tailed Hummingbird, 50 percent for the Anna's Hummingbird, and a remarkable 100 percent for the Ruby-throated Hummingbird.

Even within the tropics, a certain amount of migrational movement takes place. Banding records from Brazil show seasonal long-distance movements for some species.

Except when the journeys are over water, the pattern of movements is far from simple. Even within the same species, different types of movements can be observed. Postbreeding dispersal is often accompanied by altitudinal movements of juvenile birds into alpine grasslands rich with food, but for some species, a number of adults also join them. The remaining adults may move to lower altitudes and many will migrate out of the area altogether. This pattern of movement is adopted by the Anna's Hummingbird, which breeds in the Californian lowlands, and many birds disperse eastward as far as the Sierras after breeding before finally moving on again into New Mexico for the winter.

Within most of the hummingbird species inhabiting the Andes, altitudinal movements are probably much more common. Weather conditions and availability of food sources are conditions that the birds need to exploit, so altitudinal migration is essential for survival.

44

Opposite: The Ruby-throated Hummingbird (*Archilochus colubris*) is able to migrate 500 miles nonstop over the Gulf of Mexico.

Left: The Anna's Hummingbird (*Calypte anna*) increases its body weight by 50 percent before embarking on a long migration.

Scientific Study of Hummingbirds

It is only by the close study and observation of hummingbirds that their true status can be determined. Hummingbirds are small and difficult to observe, and this raises many problems for the scientists trying to learn about them. The study of movement and migration requires that birds be marked individually so that they can be recognized later in their life, wherever they may be found, so at some time they must be caught. The process of trapping the birds and applying small, lightweight, individually marked rings or bands is the normal procedure. The whole process—from making the tiny ring to attaching it to the short, thin leg of a hummingbird— is a daunting task. It demands great care and patience as well as enormous skill; the bird must not be harmed or unduly disturbed from its previous

Below: A juvenile female Calliope Hummingbird (*Stellula calliope*). Only experienced, licensed bird banders are allowed to handle hummingbirds.

activities. Any serious diversion from its normal behavior would be counterproductive.

The band's small size limits the amount of information it can carry, and this is confined to a unique coded number, which also denotes its place of ringing. The band itself must have smooth edges to prevent abrasions on the leg, and when it is closed around the leg, there must be no gaps or edges that could cause it to become entangled with anything on which the bird perches.

Handling the tiny body of a living hummingbird is a task that requires special technique and care, and only a small number of dedicated banders are licensed to carry out the work. They are usually based at recognized observatories and field stations, often in areas that are known to be frequented by hummingbirds.

One such observatory is the Southeastern Arizona Bird Observatory in Bisbee, Arizona. Here, hummingbirds are caught in mist nets, which are

Below: The outside diameter of this hummingbird ring is just two millimeters—so small that at least sixty-five could fit on top of a penny.

47

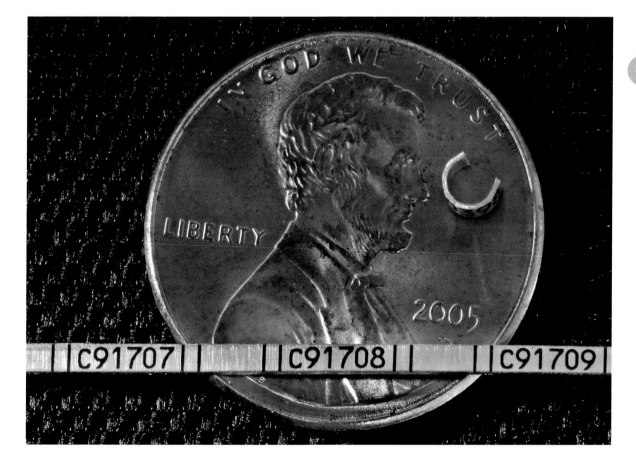

very soft, fine nets suspended on taut strings attached between two rigid poles. The nets are so fine that they are almost invisible when viewed from the front. When placed against the background of a bush and in the flight path of a bird, the bird cannot see it and is caught. It falls harmlessly into a pocket of the net and lies there for the few moments it takes for the bander to reach it. Once removed from the net, birds are identified and banded, and biometric data, including weight, size, and plumage details, are recorded. The birds are then fed from an artificial feeder while still in the bander's hand before they are released back to the wild.

The amassed data can be analyzed to study many different aspects of hummingbird biology as well as population levels, and birds retrapped in other places can contribute to our knowledge of life span, migration patterns, and movement.

Below: Attaching an identification band demands enormous skill and patience. A soft blanket is used to keep the hummingbird calm.

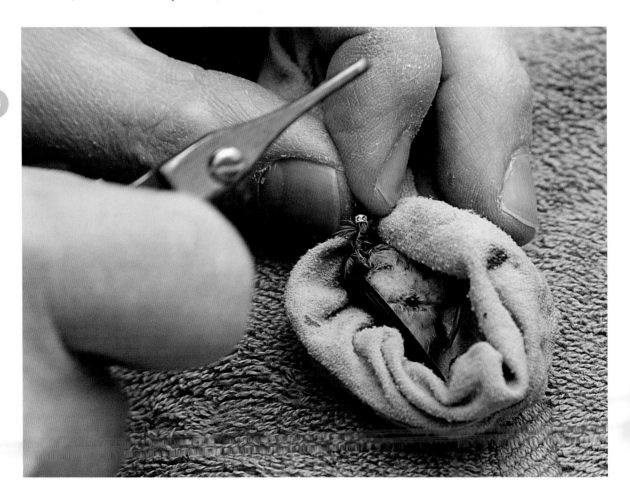

49

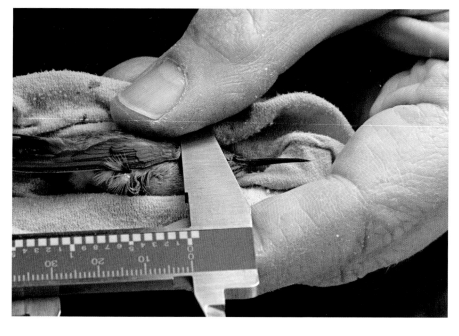

Above and left: Precise bill and wing measurememments are conducted on a Calliope Hummingbird (*Stellula calliope*).

White-tipped Sicklebill

Eutoxeres aquila • 4³/₄–5¹/₂ inches (12–14 cm)

This is a fairly common hummingbird within its range and is often known by several other names, in particular the Common, White, Brown-tailed, or Bronze Sicklebill. There are three subspecies—the nominate and more easterly *E. a. aquila* is found in the eastern Andes from northern Peru to Colombia. *E. a. heterura* ranges through the western Andes from Ecuador into southwest Colombia, while *E. a. salvini* is spread through western Colombia and up through Panama into Costa Rica. It is sedentary through most of its range, and is found more often in foothill areas where water is present, particularly in or near humid forests and forest edges. Heliconia is a favorite feeding plant, as are other plants suited to its sickle-shaped bill. It also eats spiders and various insects. This is one of the few hummingbirds that prefers to perch when feeding.

The markedly decurved bill of this hummingbird is a great aid to identification. Apart from the Buff-tailed Sicklebill *(Eutoxeres condamini)*, it has the most notably decurved bill of all hummingbirds. Fortunately, the two are easily separated by the more buffish plumage and buff tail coloring as they overlap in range in southern Colombia and Peru. The White-tipped Sicklebill has dark green upperparts, including the crown and nape. The rounded, bronze-green tail has white tips, which is more obvious in the nominate subspecies. Underparts are white-streaked black with undertail coverts edged in pale reddish-brown. The bill is blackish and the feet are brown. Females are very similar to males, although they have slightly shorter wings.

Breeding takes place from January in the north of the range through to September in the south. A suspended, cup-shaped woven nest is constructed at the tip of a drooping leaf with a mass of plant fibers and tiny rootlets bound together and onto its support by means of spiderwebs. The female incubates her two eggs for two and a half weeks and the chicks fledge about three and a half weeks later.

Hairy Hermit

Glaucis hirsuta • 4³/₄ inches (12 cm)

The other common name for this species is the Rufous-breasted Hermit, and two subspecies are recognized. The northerly subspecies, *G. h. insularum*, is isolated on the islands of Trinidad, Tobago, and Grenada. The nominate subspecies, *G. h. hirsuta*, is much more widespread, covering nearly all of Brazil apart from the far south and far northeast, as well as almost all of the remainder of northern South America east of the Andes, including the Guianas, Venezuela, Colombia, Panama, Peru, and Bolivia. This species is common over much of its range, particularly in the Amazonas. It is thought to be sedentary, keeping to the lowlands, where it can be found in a great diversity of habitats. However, it is never far from trees even when present in areas of grassland. Not only does it enjoy dense woodland and thickets, it also frequents clearings and forest edges and is often found in marshland and riverine habitats. It is a nectar feeder and seeks out flowers of trees, shrubs, and vines, and is often seen near heliconia. Small insects and spiders are also gleaned from the foliage.

The male's upperparts are bronze-green and the underparts reddish-brown, becoming brown at the chin and flanks. The underbelly is off-white. The roundish tail has white-tipped feathers; the central two are green, and the outer feathers are reddish-brown at the base with a broad black subterminal band. His slightly decurved bill is black above and buffish-orange below. The female, although similar, is much paler over the throat and upper breast, and her bill is more decurved.

The northerly subspecies has a breeding season spread over the first six months of the year, whereas for the nominate subspecies, the breeding season is more dependent on its location. A cup-shaped nest is constructed with pieces of plant fiber, leaf, and a few spiderwebs and suspended from the underside of a drooping leaf with similar materials. The whole of the outside is decorated with pieces of lichen, bark, and tiny twigs. Normally, two eggs are incubated by the female for nearly three weeks. The chicks fledge around three to four weeks later.

Green Hermit

Phaethornis guy • 5 inches (13 cm)

Known also as the Guy's Hermit or the White-tailed Hermit, there are four subspecies; the nominate, *P. g. guy*, is concentrated in Trinidad and an area of northeast Venezuela. The western subspecies, *P. g. coruscans*, is isolated in an area from northwest Colombia and through Costa Rica. *P. g. emiliae* is spread through the less mountainous regions and river valleys of northwest Colombia. *P. g. apicalis* inhabits the eastern mountain slopes of the Andes, from southern Peru up into northwest Venezuela. Although they are often seen close to forest edges and in clearings, they seem to prefer the seclusion of the denser undergrowth associated with humid forests. The birds take nectar from a wide variety of flowers, shrubs, trees, and other plants, and glean for insects and spiders.

Birds of the nominate subspecies are the largest and have mildly iridescent green upperparts and dullish bronze-green underparts tinged with gray. A blackish-green patch extends from the lore (the space between the bill and the eye) and below the eye to the ear coverts. A buffish-orange postocular stripe is sometimes evident. The upper tail coverts have an emerald-green hue leading into the base of the tail feathers, which have a broad black band across the tips. The central tail feathers of the predominantly rounded tail are slightly extended at the tips. The long, slightly decurved bill is black above, and the lower mandible is orange-brown toward the base. There is also an orange-brown gular stripe. Females usually have shorter bills and wings, and the narrow extensions of the central tail feathers are considerably longer and almost white at the tips. The outer tail feathers also have white tips. They have more obvious gular and postocular orange-buff stripes. Of all the subspecies, *P. g. coruscans* has the most brilliant plumage and even shows some iridescence on the underparts.

Breeding sites are usually close to water. A long, pendulous, conical nest is suspended from the tip of a long, drooping leaf. Plant fibers along with spiderwebs and pieces of lichen are combined in the loose cup-shaped nest and suspension. Although the males remain near the nest, it is the female that does the incubation. The two eggs hatch after two and a half weeks; the chicks take another three and a half weeks to fledge.

White-bearded Hermit

Phaethornis hispidus • 5 inches (13 cm)

Also referred to as the d'Osery's Hermit, this bird prefers the humid lowland forests east of the Andes, covering a large area of northern South America including Venezuela, Colombia, Ecuador, Peru, Bolivia, and the western Amazonas of Brazil. It is found particularly in damp locations by rivers and in swamp forests as well as near bamboo stands. It takes nectar from flowering trees, shrubs, and epiphytes and is especially attracted by heliconia. Small insects and flies are also taken by gleaning.

It is of typical hermit appearance, having bronze-green upperparts with a grayish tinge over the crown and gray edges to the upper tail coverts. The feathers of the predominantly rounded tail are dark bronze-green tipped in white, with the central two feathers extended into narrow white tips. Underparts are gray with a distinct off-white gular stripe leading up to the chin. The dark ear coverts are bordered by a white

malar stripe and another white stripe to the rear. The bill is blackish and decurved, a trait that is more accentuated in the female.

The breeding season is dependent on the location, but takes place almost throughout the year. A suspended nest of plant fibers is bound together and attached to an overhanging leaf with spiderwebs. The clutch of two eggs is incubated for about two and a half weeks; the young fledge around three weeks later.

Reddish Hermit

Phaethornis ruber • 3¹/₂ inches (9 cm)

This small hermit also takes the names of Pygmy Hermit and Red-vented Hermit. There are four subspecies distributed in the northern half of South America east of the Andes. The nominate subspecies, *P. r. ruber*, covers a band from French Guiana and Surinam through the Amazonas of Brazil and into northern Bolivia and southeastern Peru. *P. r. longipennis* is from southern Peru, *P. r. nigricinctus* is from northern Peru and northeastward through eastern Colombia and just into southern Venezuela, and *P. r. episcopus* is spread through central and eastern Venezuela eastward to French Guiana and south into northern Brazil. It is another fairly common lowland species that lives in or near forests. Nectar is taken both by hover-feeding and piercing the flower base. Numerous insects are also gleaned from foliage.

The male has an iridescent bronze-green forehead, crown, nape, mantle, and wing coverts. The underparts and rump are reddish-brown, and there is a dark band, sometimes almost black, across the breast. His nearly black ear coverts are bordered at the rear by a whitish stripe and at the front by a thin white malar stripe. Rufous upper tail coverts lead into rounded tail feathers that are reddish-brown at the base and darker toward a black subterminal band, with a narrow tip of pale rufous. His decurved bill is mainly black, but is pale rufous at the base of the lower mandible. The female is paler on the underparts, with a less obvious dark patch in the center of the breast, and her slightly longer tail feathers have broader rufous tips.

Breeding takes place from May to October; the season varies considerably with location. The nest, a suspended cone shape with the cup at the base, is usually attached to the underside of a long, pendulous leaf. Spiderwebs are used to attach the nest to the leaf and to bind together the plant fibers, lichen, moss, and leaf pieces. The female incubates her two eggs for just over two weeks, and the young fledge some two and a half to three weeks later.

Green-fronted Lancebill

Doryfera ludovicae • 5 inches (13 cm)

This species inhabits the humid forests and wet cloud forests of Costa Rica and Panama as well as the Andes from western Venezuela in the north through Colombia, Ecuador, and Peru down into northwest Bolivia. The subspecies *D. l. veraguensis* is found in an area from the northern central part of Costa Rica eastward to western Panama, and the nominate subspecies is found elsewhere in the range. During the breeding season, the Green-fronted Lancebill prefers to remain within the forest, seeking out nectar from the long, tubular flowers of epiphytes to which it is so well adapted. However, after breeding it begins to explore outside the forest canopy, along the edges and in clearings wherever the long, tubular flowers are present. Not only does it take nectar from the flowers by hovering beneath them, it will also glean insects and spiders from foliage in a similar manner. Sometimes it even hawks for flying insects.

This species has a comparatively long and slightly upturned black bill, and the forehead is brilliant iridescent green. The crown, nape, and sides of the head are iridescent copper-brown, becoming coppery-green on the back down to the blue-gray rump. The dark gray to black rounded tail has pale grayish tips, and the underparts are a dull bronze-green. Females usually have a smaller iridescent forehead patch that is sometimes missing altogether.

The breeding season starts in late July and runs to January. The cup-shaped nest, made of mosses, plant fibers, and pieces of tree fern bound together with spiderwebs, is attached to a suspended rootlet or twig, most often in a shaded position. Two eggs are typically incubated for about two and a half weeks, with the young fledging almost a month later.

Violet Sabrewing

Campylopterus hemileucurus • 5³/₄ inches (15 cm)

Another common name for this brilliantly colored hummingbird is the de Lattre's Sabrewing. The nominate and more northerly of the two subspecies, *C. h. hemileucurus*, is found in an area of the central highlands stretching from southern Chiapas in Mexico through Guatemala, Honduras, and Nicaragua to the border of Costa Rica, although other isolated populations exist in northern Guatemala and southern Mexico. *C. h. mellitus* ranges from western Costa Rica to western Panama. Throughout its range, this large hummingbird has adapted well to the changes brought about by humans and is now found close to human habitation in yards, gardens, plantations, and farmland. Its main habitat, however, lies on the mountain slopes and foothills, where the birds are close to the edges of a humid forest. They are also frequently seen in riverine habitats by streams. Within forests, it keeps below the canopy, seeking out flowers of shrubs and vines in search of nectar. It also takes numerous insects and spiders by foraging through undergrowth and gleaning from foliage and occasionally snatching flies from the air.

The male has a brilliant violet-blue breast, throat, nape, and upper back, and the lower back is dark green. The forehead also has a green tinge. The mainly dark blue-black tail is squarish and has broad white tips on the outer three feathers, which are visible in flight. The wings are brownish-black with obviously more substantial shafts to the first two primary feathers, creating the shape of a saber. There is a white spot at the rear of the eye, and the black bill is decurved. The female lacks the violet coloring and has greenish upperparts that become bronze-green on the crown. Her breast is gray leading up to a violet throat. She also has a more decurved bill than the male. The male of *C. h. mellitus* is much more violet than the violet-blue of the nominate subspecies.

Breeding occurs during the wet season when a substantial nest of moss is constructed on a thin, horizontal branch overhanging water. The moss is neatly interwoven with plant fibers and bound together with spiderwebs. No further reliable breeding information is available.

White-necked Jacobin

Florisuga mellivora • 4³/₄ inches (12 cm)

Other common names for this medium-sized hummingbird are the Collared Hummingbird and the Jacobin. There are two subspecies; the more confined and slightly larger subspecies, *F. m. flabellifera*, is found only on Tobago. The nominate subspecies, *F. m. mellivora*, however, has a broad range from southern Mexico eastward to Panama and Colombia, and is also spread over most of the Amazonas southward to Matto Grosso and eastward to Goyaz and Maranhao, taking in the Guianas and Trinidad. More often found in the lowlands, it sometimes ventures into the foothills but seldom above 5,000 feet. It prefers high trees, both in plantations or humid forests, but is frequently found in open woodland and secondary forests. Although it regularly hawks for insects and flies, it feeds mainly on nectar from flowering trees and shrubs and can frequently be seen at flowering epiphytes and heliconia.

The male has an outstanding dark blue head, neck, and chest. Between the nape and upper back is a distinct white collar. The rest of the upperparts are a brilliant dark green stretching down over the rump to extended upper tail coverts. The belly is white, as is the squarish tail, which has a narrow black terminal band. The very slightly decurved bill is black. The typical female plumage has all-green upperparts and a whitish belly. The breast and throat feathers often appear mainly green with fine whitish edges forming a regular pattern, but this can be variable. The tail feathers, including the extended upper tail coverts, are a dark green-blue with fine white tips.

The breeding season is variable throughout the range but occurs mainly at the end of the dry season and into the wet season. Nest sites are frequently chosen where there is protection from above, such as a large leaf, but are frequently only a few feet above the ground. Very fine plant fibers are bound together with spiderwebs into a small, bowl-shaped nest. No other breeding information is available.

Green Violet-ear

Colibri thalassinus • 4¹/₂ inches (11¹/₂ cm)

This species includes subspecies that have, in the past, been considered as individual species in their own right. *C. t. cyanotus* was previously called the Mountain Violet-ear and *C. t. thalassinus*, now the nominate subspecies, was called the Mexican Violet-ear. The nominate and more northerly subspecies, *C. t. thalassinus*, occasionally found in the far southeastern United States, ranges mainly from central Mexico southward and well into northern Nicaragua. From there, *C. t. cabanidis* can be found, and its range extends farther south through Costa Rica and into the hills of western Panama. The range of *C. t. cyanotus* covers the mountainous regions of Ecuador, Colombia, and Venezuela. The most southerly subspecies, *C. t. crissalis*, keeps to the Andes through Peru and Bolivia and down into northern Argentina. Although primarily a mountain species, these birds are also found at lower altitudes, particularly when dispersing after the breeding season. They prefer a more open habitat with a scattering of trees and shrubs, but can often be found close to farms and pastureland, sometimes venturing into plantations, yards, and gardens with a profusion of flowering shrubs. Besides feeding from nectar, they frequently take spiders and small insects, either by gleaning them from hedgerows or by hawking.

The plumage of the nominate subspecies is predominantly iridescent bluish-green with blackish wings and a glittering dark blue-green patch on the upper breast. At the lower breast and vent, the plumage becomes dull gray. Iridescent blue-green feathers of the throat, often extending down into the breast, have blackish spots in their centers. The ear coverts, which extend down to the neck, are a dark violet that glistens silver-blue in certain lights. The bluish green coloring of the back continues down into the central feathers of the rather square tail; the outer tail feathers appear more turquoise-blue. There is a dark

subterminal band across all of the tail. The slightly curved bill and the feet are black. Females may appear a little less bright in plumage and are slightly smaller in size. The plumage of other subspecies, although very similar, lack the dark blue-green patch on the upper breast.

The breeding season can be from July through March depending on local conditions, but usually coincides with the end of the wet season. The substantial cup-shaped nest, often low down, is frequently positioned precariously on a thin twig or root. Fine grasses, moss, plant down, and bits of tree fern are all bound together with spiderwebs and lined with fine plant fibers before being decorated externally with lichen and fragments of leaf and bark. Two eggs are incubated for around two and a half weeks, and the young can take as long as four weeks to fledge.

Sparkling Violet-ear

Colibri coruscans • 5-5½ inches (13–14 cm)

Also known by the common names of Chequered, Gould's, and Colombian Violet-ear, the species has only two subspecies. The nominate subspecies, *C. c. coruscans*, ranges from the northwest tip of Venezuela through western Colombia, Ecuador, and Peru into western Bolivia and the northwest of Argentina. The subspecies *C. c. germanus* is found in northern South America, across southern Venezuela eastward to Guiana, taking in the northern fringes of Brazil.

This is a species that prefers a habitat of open woodland and forest edges and is frequently seen close to human habitation in plantations and yards. It is also found in ornamental gardens in large cities. Birds found at low elevations tend to be sedentary, with only small dispersal movements after breeding. At higher elevations, it inhabits areas prolific in pàramo plants, often more than 5,500 feet above sea level. These birds migrate to lower elevations during the dry season when the food plants become scarce. It has adapted to a wide range of food plants and feeds from ground level to the treetops. Its basic diet is flower nectar supplemented with insects gleaned from plants or hawked in the air.

Male birds have bluish-green upperparts with a metallic sheen. The underparts are the same color, but there is a bluish patch in the center of the belly and also under the chin. The dark blue ear coverts consist of extended feathers, which can be raised in display. The dark tail is a metallic blue-green with a suggestion of a darker blue subterminal band. Females have similar coloration and also a small white spot just behind the eye. The subspecies *C. c. germanus* can be distinguished by its bluer underparts and tail and the area at the front of the crown.

Breeding occurs from early July through October. The nest, often on top of a horizontal branch or in a cavity among rocks, is cup-shaped, consisting of fine plant fibers decorated externally with pieces of lichen and small twigs, although some birds create a suspended structure from the end of a branch. The female incubates a clutch of two eggs for up to eighteen days. The young fledge after three weeks in the nest.

Black-throated Mango

Anthracothorax nigricollis • 4¹/₂–4³/₄ inches (11–12 cm)

The range of this species is vast, covering the greater part of northern South America from western Panama to the Guianas, including Trinidad and Tobago in the north, to south Brazil, taking in much of Peru, Bolivia, Paraguay, and the north of Argentina. This is one of the more common species of hummingbirds in the tropical areas of its range, especially at low elevations, where it can even be seen in cities. It likes a more open habitat with a few trees and shrubs—often very close to human habitation. Gardens, yards, and parkland are visited frequently, as well as agricultural land, but it can also be found on the lower cultivated hillsides. It takes nectar from tall, flowering trees and shrubs and also hawks for insects.

The upperparts of the male and female are both bright bronze-green. The male has a dense black strip from the chin to the breast, which is edged with iridescent blue-green, particularly at the neck, and green at the flanks. The central tail feathers are bronze-green with black edges, and the outer feathers are reddish-brown with a purple sheen and finely edged in blue toward the tips. His black bill is lightly decurved. The female is very similar to the male but lacks the blue-green border to the black breast stripe. Instead, she has a white border running from the base of the bill right down the flanks. Her tail is also similar to that of the male but has a dark, almost black subterminal band and whitish tips.

Breeding takes place during the first six months of the year, and a nest site is chosen high in trees on top of an exposed branch. The cup-shaped nest, consisting of fine plant fibers and a few spiderwebs, is decorated externally with pieces of lichen. The female incubates her two eggs for two and a half weeks; the young fledge about three and a half weeks later. This species often attempts two broods in a season.

Green-breasted Mango

Anthracothorax prevostii • 4¹/₂–5¹/₂ inches (11–14 cm)

Found in southern Mexico and Central America, this medium-sized hummingbird has also been spotted in the lower Rio Grande Valley of southern Texas. It inhabits tropical deciduous forest as well as open areas of shrubs, gardens, and plantations. It searches out flowers from a wide variety of trees, shrubs, and vines to feed on nectar. It also gleans over foliage for insects, steals from spiderwebs, and hawks for flying insects from the treetops.

The longish black bill is slightly decurved. The adult male has glittering green upperparts with a dark area under the chin that becomes blue-green on the throat. The tail feathers are deep magenta, tipped with black. The two central tail feathers are bronze-green. Females and immature males have bronze-green upperparts and white underparts.

During the long breeding season, which starts as early as October and runs through May, only a single brood is attempted. The tiny, cup-shaped nest, built of plant fibers and down and disguised on the outside with pieces of lichen, is usually located high in trees, attached to an upright stem. The clutch of two eggs takes a little over two weeks to incubate; the young fledge some three to four weeks later.

Ruby Topaz

Chrysolampis mosquitus • 3¼-3½ inches (8-9 cm)

Known as just the Ruby Topaz, this is one of the better known of the hummingbirds. It has brilliant coloration and was at one time exported throughout the world from Brazil for the pet trade. It also has a widespread distribution over the northern part of South America, extending down in the east through most of northern and central Brazil and into eastern Bolivia. It is also found throughout the islands that fringe the north coast, from Trinidad and Tobago in the east to Aruba in the west. Breeding birds prefer the lowland regions with open grassland and scattered trees, as well as cultivated land and gardens.

They seek out nectar-bearing flowers from a wide variety of plants, shrubs, trees, and cacti both wild and cultivated, and also hawk for insects and glean along hedgerows for small spiders.

The brilliance of color reflected by this bird's iridescent plumage is particularly noticeable. Males have a ruby-red crown and nape sometimes tinged with orange and a brightly iridescent warm yellow upper breast. In some birds the upper breast is greenish. The back, lower breast, and underparts are dark brown with an olive sheen, and the tail is a dark chestnut with a black tip. Females lack the bright iridescent red and yellow of the male's head and breast and have mainly olive-green upperparts and

off-white underparts. Birds from Trinidad and Tobago occasionally have a small, elongated, iridescent green throat patch. The central tail feathers are olive-green, whereas the remainder are chestnut with a dark subterminal band and white tips.

The birds of the Caribbean islands and more northerly regions choose to breed from December to June, whereas those from the south in Brazil start some two months earlier, finishing in January. Their very ornate and tiny cup-shaped nest is a mass of fine plant fibers bound up with spiderwebs and covered externally with pieces of moss, lichen, and small bark flakes. It is secured in the fork of a tree or shrub, usually six to nine feet above the ground and occasionally much higher. Normally two eggs are laid, and are incubated for a little over two weeks; the young fledge in about three weeks.

Tufted Coquette

Lophornis ornatus • 2³/₄ inches (7 cm)

This small hummingbird is also known as the Splendid Coquette, and is found not only on Trinidad but also over a large area covering the Guianas and taking in eastern Venezuela and part of northern Brazil north of the Amazon. It is a sedentary species, living in a wide variety of habitats but keeping more to open areas such as savannas, thickets, forest edges, and even plantations and farmland close to human habitation. It seems to prefer more lowland areas but is also seen in mountainous regions. It relies mainly on nectar from a wide variety of flowers, but also catches insects and spiders by gleaning, and sometimes hawks for flies.

Although found in a completely separate region, the male Tufted Coquette can be confused with several of the other coquettes; the main difference is its long, pale rufous fan of feathers that emanates from behind the cheek. Each of these feathers terminates in a green iridescent spot. Females differ in having almost all-rufous underparts. Like the Frilled Coquette (*Lophornis magnificus*), the male has a long, dark rufous crest that rises from an iridescent green forehead. The upperparts are a bright iridescent green set off by a white band across the top of the bronze-tinged rump. The central feathers of the rather straight tail are also bronze-green; the outer feathers are rufous. The gorget is a shining emerald-green contrasting with lighter green underparts. His short, straight bill is black with a red tip. The female lacks the crest and elongated cheek feathers, and has all-green upperparts except for a buffish-white rump band and bronze rump. Her tail feathers are tipped with pale rufous, and her bill is reddish-brown with a black tip.

Breeding occurs mainly in the dry season when a nest is built low down on a branch. It is made from a mixture of plant fibers often intermixed with pieces of moss and spiderwebs. Two eggs are incubated by the female for two weeks; the young take up to three weeks to fledge.

Frilled Coquette

Lophornis magnificus • 3 inches (7¹/₂ cm)

The range of this species covers an area bounded by the east coast of Brazil from Santa Catarina in the south almost to San Salvador in the north, and then westward in an arc, taking in Goiás and part of Mato Grosso. Their preferred habitat is the edge of humid forests, but they will readily accept man-made habitats such as plantations and areas of secondary growth. They also take readily to parks, yards, and gardens well stocked with flowering plants. Nectar from smaller flowering plants seems to be the most attractive to this species, although they also consume small insects and spiders.

The male has bronze-green upperparts, and both the forehead and throat are an iridescent emerald-green. The green crown is covered by a distinct long russet crest that extends backward way over the neck. Feathers extending from the throat and behind the chin form a fan shape. Each feather, which is white and terminates in a narrow, iridescent green band, can give the appearance of a series of concentric crescents. There is a distinct white band across the top of the rump, the rather square tail and upper tail coverts are bronze-colored, and the underparts are gray-green. The relatively short and straight bill is red tipped in black. Females have neither the crest nor ear tufts, and apart from dull gray-green underparts, the rest of the plumage is similar to the male's, but not as

bright. Her forehead and crown are tinged red, and the throat is off-white with a fine pattern of rufous and dark brown crescents. The tail feathers are also slightly different, as they are more rufous at the tail coverts and change to dark bronze toward the end, but are tipped with pale rufous spots.

Breeding occurs from August to mid-March, when a cup-shaped nest is constructed from moss, plant fibers, and down, then decorated externally with small pieces of lichen. The female incubates two eggs for a little under two weeks; the young fledge in about three weeks.

Black-crested Coquette

Lophornis helenae • 2³/₄ inches (7 cm)

Also known as the Princess Helena's Coquette, this small hummingbird prefers a somewhat open lowland and foothill habitat, particularly at forest edges. Its main range forms a band from Veracruz in southern Mexico eastward through northern Oaxaca, northern Chiapas, northern Guatemala, and then along the northern coast of Honduras and Nicaragua through to eastern Costa Rica. Another population is spread through the Pacific lowlands of Guatemala. It feeds mainly on nectar from flowering trees and shrubs, and gleans insects and spiders from foliage and branches.

The male of this species has an iridescent green crown that extends backward in long, thin, hairlike black feathers. The upperparts are bronze-green from the back of the head down to the central tail feathers apart from a pale, buff-orange band that carries right across the top of the slightly blackish-green rump. The tail is forked, and the orange-buff outer feathers have blackish-green edges. The gorget is a bright iridescent green bordered on the upper breast by a dark band. The remainder of the underparts are white with iridescent bronze-colored spots. The three extended feathers at the lower rear edge of the gorget are dark on the outer web and buff on the inner. He has a short red bill with a black tip. The female has no crest; her crown is bronze-green. She does not have the green gorget and extended cheek feathers of the male. Instead, she has white underparts covered in small iridescent bronze spots apart from a bronze band across the upper breast. Her undertail coverts are russet-cinnamon, and the outer tail feathers have a broad green-black subterminal band.

It is thought that this species nests well above the ground; however, no reliable breeding information is available.

Wire-crested Thorntail

Discosura popelairii • male: 4¹/₂ inches (11¹/₂ cm), female: 3 inches (7¹/₂ cm)

Also known as the Popelair's Coquette, this seemingly rare species is usually found in the humid forests of the foothills east of the Andes in an arc ranging from central Colombia in the north through eastern Ecuador and southward into central Peru. It is one of those birds of which little is known because of its apparently shy habits and its tendency to remain high in the tree canopy. It does not adapt well to man-made habitats and is therefore likely to suffer from destruction of natural forest bordering on its current range. It feeds on nectar from flowering trees, in particular the inga, and it also gleans for insects and spiders.

Its name aptly describes the outstanding feature of the male—a long crest of thin, almost hairlike plumes balanced at the other end of its body by a tail of equally narrow but longer feathers. These are shown off to their best in display when the crest is pushed forward along with the tail to confront the female. The crown, crest, and throat of the male are an iridescent green, as is the upper mantle, whereas the nape and back have a copper-green tinge. Across the top of the rump is a distinct white band, below which the rump becomes blackish-blue in the center, with small areas of green at the sides. The blackish-blue tail feathers all show white shafts. The breast is a dark brown that becomes white at the vent. The wings are black, as is the short, straight bill. The female lacks the crest plumes and the long tail of the male, but otherwise has similarly colored upperparts. She has a dark throat patch, finely speckled white, and a distinct white malar stripe. Her slightly forked tail has white-tipped feathers.

Very little is known of its breeding habits except that it occurs around April and its chosen nest sites are on very high branches.

79

Red-billed Streamertail

Trochilus polytmus • Male: 11³/₄ inches (30 cm), Female: 4¹/₄ inches (10¹/₂ cm)

Other names for this spectacular bird are the Western Streamertail and the Jamaican Doctor Bird. It is quite a common species throughout Jamaica, except in the very east of the island, where it is replaced by the Black-billed Streamertail (*Trochilus scitulus*). It readily occupies areas close to human habitation, such as yards, gardens, parks, and farmland. It seems to be more numerous at an altitude of about 3,000 feet, where it forages around clearings and forest edges, but can be found at higher altitudes when the birds disperse after breeding. Not only does it take nectar from a wide variety of flowering plants, it also takes many insects by gleaning through foliage or even from spiderwebs. It frequently hawks for aerial insects and has a habit of visiting and licking sap from holes in trees made by woodpeckers, in addition to extracting nectar from flowers previously pierced at their base by Bananaquits (*Coereba flaveola*).

Apart from the male's black head and the feathers of the extended crown, nape, and ear coverts, his main body plumage is a bright iridescent emerald-green. The deeply forked tail is black, with the second outer feathers extended to form long streamers that are typically crossed when perched. The edges of these two feathers are corrugated on the inner webs, giving a crinkled appearance. His almost straight bill is pinkish-red with a black tip. The female lacks the black plumage of the male and has all-green upperparts. Her white underparts become spotted with green at the flanks, while her short, forked tail has green feathers at the center—the dark blue outer feathers are clearly tipped white.

Breeding seems to take place throughout the year, and as many as three broods are frequently attempted. A low nest site is usually chosen, on a thin branch or plant frond. The cup-shaped nest, mainly of fine plant fibers, is interwoven with spiderwebs and decorated with small pieces of lichen. The female incubates her two eggs for almost three weeks, and it takes about another three weeks before the young fledge.

Blue-chinned Sapphire

Chlorostilbon notatus • 3–3¹/₂ inches (8–9 cm)

Another common name for this species is the Audebert's Hummingbird. There are three subspecies known at present, although it has in the past been speculated that there are more. However, it is now thought that the others could be hybrids with other hummingbird species. The range covered is northern South America. *C. n. notatus* is found along a broad coastal belt from eastern Colombia through Venezuela and the Guianas right around to the eastern tip of Brazil, also taking in Trinidad and Tobago. *C. n. puruensis* covers an area to the north of the Amazon, from the northeast tip of Peru through western Colombia and southern Venezuela to the river Trombetas. The much smaller area covered by *C. n. obsoletus* is in northeast Peru. All are thought to be sedentary, with only small movements due to dispersal after breeding.

It feeds on nectar, depending on low flowering plants and bushes, but it also eats numerous insects and spiders, which it gleans from hedgerows and hawks in the air. It appears to be quite a common species, probably because of its feeding habits. It is regularly seen in city parks and gardens, as well as in domestic yards and around cultivated land. Woodland edges and savanna are other favorite haunts.

Males have upperparts that are a metallic bronze-green and underparts of green slightly tinted with blue at the throat and yellow on the breast. The forked tail is gray-blue. The shortish, straight red bill has a black tip. Females are similar but show white underparts with iridescent green spots, particularly on the throat and breast.

Its breeding season occurs from late July to November. The nest site is often very close to the ground, usually about three feet up, on top of a slender branch or root. The tiny, cup-shaped nest consists of fine plant fibers bound together with spiderwebs and decorated with pieces of leaf, lichen, small twigs, and bark. The lining is usually the downy fibers from seeding plants. The female incubates two eggs for just over two weeks, and the young fledge after another three weeks.

Glittering-bellied Emerald

Chlorostilbon aureoventris • 3–4$\frac{1}{8}$ inches (9$\frac{1}{2}$–10$\frac{1}{2}$ cm)

Also known as the Pucheran's Emerald, there are four subspecies, all sedentary. The subspecies *C. a. pucherani* is found only in the east of Brazil and is slightly smaller than the nominate subspecies, *C. a. aureoventris,* which exists through Paraguay, Bolivia, and the area of Brazil bordering those two countries. *C. a. igneus* lives in northwest Argentina and *C. a. berlepschi* ranges through southern Brazil and Uruguay to the northeastern part of Argentina. Its range covers a broad spectrum of habitats, from the tropical and subtropical forest margins of the Andean foothills in Bolivia to semidesert, dry savanna, and grassland regions. It can often be found in city parks and yards, where it forages through the treetops for nectar from flowers and fruit. It can occasionally be seen hawking among swarms of small insects.

The nominate subspecies has dark green upperparts with a golden tinge, blending into a paler green band of upper tail coverts that merge into a slightly forked, dark gray-blue tail. The breast and belly are bright iridescent bronze-green, becoming blue toward the throat. Both the forehead and crown are bronze-green. The bill is red with a black tip. Females' upperparts and head are slightly yellower than those of the males, and they also have a grayish-white streak trailing back behind the eye. Her underparts lack the green of the males, and are white turning to a whitish-buff at the breast and lower belly.

The main breeding season is from August to mid-November, when a tiny, cup-shaped nest is built on a small branch close to the ground. Plant fibers along with strips of dry leaf and sometimes bark are held together with spiderwebs. It is usually lined with fine fibers from seeding plants, and the outside is frequently decorated with other local plant debris. The female incubates her two eggs for two weeks; it is another three weeks before the young fledge.

Cuban Emerald

Chlorostilbon ricordii • Male: 4¹/₂ inches (11¹/₂ cm), Female: 4 inches (10 cm)

Distributed throughout Cuba, the Isle of Pines, and the northern Bahamas, where it is found in the lowlands, the Cuban Emerald also occasionally appears as a vagrant in the southernmost tip of Florida. It does not seem to be associated with any particular type of habitat, as it is found in both dry open countryside and humid forests, although it is more prevalent in areas containing low shrubs. It is also common close to human habitation in yards, parks, and plantations where a succession of flowering shrubs are present. Nectar is a main food source, along with insects and small spiders caught either by gleaning or hawking.

Males have a shining bronze-green plumage, with the throat and breast iridescent green and undertail coverts light gray to white. The area covering the forehead and crown often has a darker and duller appearance. There is a small white spot behind the eye. The dark, forked tail has a metallic bronze sheen, and the wings are black but tinged green. The slightly curved bill is mainly black, with the lower mandible showing signs of red on the underside toward the base. Females are similar, although they lack the iridescent green underparts, having a buff white throat and breast that becomes iridescent green at the flanks. Females have a larger and longer white spot behind the eye, a less forked tail sometimes tipped white, and white undertail coverts.

Breeding takes place throughout the year. A low site, frequently located among vines but also in the outer branches of low trees, is chosen for the cup-shaped nest, which is a construction of fine plant fibers, moss, and thin bark strips bound together with spiderwebs. The outside of the nest is decorated with tiny pieces of lichen or bark fragments. The female incubates two eggs for just over two weeks, and the young fledge around three weeks later.

Puerto Rican Emerald

Chlorostilbon maugaeus • Male: 3¹/₂ inches (9 cm), Female: 3 inches (7¹/₂ cm)

Also known as the Antillean Emerald, this hummingbird can be found throughout the island of Cuba, from the mountaintops down to the coast. Its preferred habitats seem to be associated with woodland, trees, and large shrubs, whether they be forests, open woodland, or plantations. A wide range of flowering trees and shrubs are exploited for their nectar, and tree canopies are gleaned for insects and spiders.

The upperparts, nape, crown, forehead, lower belly, and undertail coverts are a dark iridescent green that contrasts with the bright iridescent blue-green of the throat patch. The forked tail is dark blue with a brilliant sheen, and the wings are black. The smaller female differs in plumage apart from the green upperparts, nape, crown, and forehead. This coloration continues down her back and through the tail coverts to halfway along the tail, where it blends into a black-brown band before ending at the white-tipped tail feathers. Her tail is only slightly forked.

Although nesting takes place throughout the year, the main breeding season is from late February through May. Tiny, cup-shaped nests are constructed in low shrubs and trees using mainly plant fibers and a lining of plant down. The outside is frequently disguised with small pieces of lichen and leaf. The female incubates her two eggs for a little over two weeks, and it is another three weeks before the young fledge.

Fiery-throated Hummingbird

Panterpe insignis • 4¹/₄ inches (11 cm)

Also called the Irazu Hummingbird, there are two subspecies—both prefer the mountain forests and cloud forests of Costa Rica. They are also frequently seen outside the forest, around the edges and in clearings, as well as in areas of grassland where dense pockets of trees remain. The nominate subspecies, *P. i. insignis*, is found from central Costa Rica eastward to the border with Panama, whereas *P. i. eisenmanni* remains in the north. They have a wide variety of flowering food plants from which to obtain nectar, including trees, shrubs, epiphytes, vines, and herbs. Besides hovering to feed, they are known to pierce holes in the base of longer blooms and to make use of holes made by other birds or insects to obtain the nectar. Insects and flies are also taken in flight by hawking.

The males and females have similar plumage. The upperparts are a brilliant dark green, becoming glittering dark blue on the forehead and crown. The tail coverts are graded from green to dark blue and then into a blue-black, rather square tail. The lores are black and an area of greenish-black extends around the ear coverts and over the nape. There is a small white spot behind the eye. The throat is a mixture of brilliant iridescent spots of color, from an orange-red at the center grading through yellow to bright green at the sides. Below the throat is an equally brilliant patch of emerald-green and purple, surrounded below and at the sides by bright green. The upper mandible is black, and the lower mandible pink. The northern Costa Rican subspecies differs in that it is smaller and has more blue on the rump and breast.

Breeding takes place between late summer and January, when a bulky nest is attached to a twig some ten feet above the ground. Plant down and moss are intermixed with spiderwebs and decorated with lichen and tree fern pieces. Only two eggs are laid, taking some two and a half weeks to incubate.

Coppery-headed Emerald

Elvira cupreiceps • 3 inches (7¹/₂ cm)

This small hummingbird breeds in a relatively confined area of the Costa Rican highlands but then descends into the lowlands. It prefers the cooler and wetter forests during the breeding season from October to March, but it can also be found in more open country with copses and scattered mature trees as well as secondary growth, plantations, and shrubbery. Nectar from flowering trees, shrubs, and epiphytes make up its diet, along with many insects and spiders gleaned from foliage as well as flies caught by hawking.

The male's plumage is distinctly coppery over the crown and upper tail coverts, and bronze-green over the nape, back, and wing coverts. The forehead is iridescent yellow-bronze, and the throat, neck, and breast are bright iridescent green. In some areas, the male has a purple spot around the middle of the breast. The vent and undertail coverts are white. The inner tail feathers are a gray-bronze, and the white outer tail feathers are tipped with gray spots. It has an obviously decurved black bill that shows a little pink at the base of the lower mandible. The female is duller and greener, with off-white underparts that have green spots at the flanks.

Breeding is from late October through March, when a nest is constructed low down in a shrub from soft plant fibers. The compact cup shape is held together with spiderwebs and decorated with moss, lichen, and scales of tree fern. Apart from the clutch size of two eggs, there is little other breeding information.

Stripe-tailed Hummingbird

Eupherusa eximia • 4 inches (10 cm)

The three subspecies of the Stripe-tailed Hummingbird are from three separate areas of the highlands from southern Mexico eastward to western Panama. *E. e. nelsoni* is the more westerly, concentrated in the mountains west of Veracruz. The nominate subspecies, *E. e. eximia*, ranges from western Chiapas through Guatemala and Honduras into central Nicaragua. *E. e. egregia* is from the mountains of Costa Rica eastward and into western Panama. They are fairly common within their range and mainly sedentary, with only small altitudinal movements before and after breeding. Mainly a forest dweller, keeping to the edges and canopy, it often ventures out into more open habitats, especially in association with riverine habitats where pockets of dense shrub and secondary growth exist. It searches out flowers from a variety of trees, shrubs, and epiphytes to obtain nectar, often piercing the flower base of the longer, bell-shaped blooms. Spiders and insects are gleaned from foliage, and flies are caught in midair.

Males have green upperparts and underparts, with a bronze sheen on the head and back, and a spotted iridescence on the breast. The slightly rounded tail is blackish-green; the two outer feathers are white at the base and tipped black with black edges to the outer webs. The wing has black primaries and reddish secondaries. The short, straight bill is black. Females are a buff-gray over the underparts, with green spotting at the flanks. The red coloring of the secondaries is less extensive and not so bright, and the black outer edges of the tail feathers are much narrower and often missing altogether.

Breeding starts as the wet season is coming to an end, when a nest site is chosen, often close to water but within the seclusion of dense woodland. The nest is constructed of very fine plant fibers and pieces of moss and lichen held together with spiderwebs and further decorated with lichen and moss. Little other breeding information is available.

Broad-billed Hummingbird

Cynanthus latirostris • 3¹/₂–4 inches (9–10 cm)

There are five subspecies; the most northerly, *C. l. magicus*, is found from southern Arizona and southwest New Mexico southward into the mountains of Nayarit in western central Mexico. Off the coast of Mexico, west of Nayarit, lie the islands Las Tres Marias, where *C. l. lawrencei*, or Lawrence's Hummingbird, is found. *C. l. latirostris* ranges from the northeast Mexican coast down through Tamaulipas and San Luis Potosi and into Veracruz. To the west of central Mexico, *C. l. propinquus* is spread through Michoacan up to Guanajuato. *C. l. doubledayi,* or the Doubleday's Hummingbird, is found along the Pacific coast of southern Mexico, taking in Chiapas, Oaxaca, and Guerrero. The southern subspecies are resident, but birds from the northerly subspecies migrate southward after breeding. The northerly subspecies, particularly those in the United States, are often found in ravines, canyons, and deserts where there is abundant plant growth. In Mexico, they are more likely to be found in dry shrubby and open areas with scattered trees. Food sources include nectar from flowering shrubs, cacti, and succulents, as well as spiders and insects gleaned from foliage.

Males are iridescent green on the crown, nape, and back, with a blue or violet-blue throat. The underparts are a shining bronze-green leading into buff-white undertail coverts. The notched tail is blue-black. Females have dull yellow-green upperparts leading into a blue-green tail with a black subterminal band and a white tip. Her underparts are gray-buff, as are her ear coverts. To the rear of the ear coverts is a white stripe. She has a black upper mandible and red lower mandible, while the male's bill is red with a black tip. Males of the subspecies *C. l. doubledayi* have generally darker plumage with iridescent dark turquoise foreheads and black undertail coverts. *C. l. magicus* has a green throat, while *C. l. lawrencei* has turquoise.

Breeding takes place from April to September in the north of the range. The cup-shaped nest decorated with pieces of leaf and bark is usually sited low down on top of a horizontal branch. Two eggs are incubated by the female for two to three weeks; the young fledge about three weeks later.

Blue-headed Hummingbird

Cyanophaia bicolor • 4¹/₂ inches (11 cm)

Another common name for this species, found in Martinique and Dominica, is the Wagler's Woodnymph. It is sedentary and found mainly in more mountainous terrain, especially within primary rain forests and at forest edges abutting rivers and streams. Not a common species, it is susceptible to the ravages of weather, particularly the hurricanes that often devastate the area. Populations of the species therefore fluctuate considerably. It consumes nectar from a wide variety of flowering plants, from trees to herbs, and also forages for insects and spiders among foliage and hawks for flies in the air.

The male is identified by his iridescent violet-blue head, including the chin and throat, and the rest of the iridescent body plumage is green, apart from dark blue upper tail coverts. The flight feathers are black and the forked tail is blue-black. His straight bill is all black apart from the base of the lower mandible, which is reddish-pink. The female is quite different, having all bright bronze-green upperparts, including the forehead and crown right down to the top half of the tail. Her central tail feathers are tipped dark blue, and the outer feathers are a finely tipped white with a dark blue subterminal band. Underparts are pale buff-gray, becoming bronze-green at the flanks.

The short breeding season is from March to May, when a nest site is chosen—usually fairly close to the ground on thin branches or even on ferns. The small, cup-shaped nest is constructed from soft, silky plant fibers, sometimes incorporating spiderwebs but usually decorated with pieces of leaf and other plant debris. The female incubates the two eggs for a little over two weeks, and the young take some three weeks to fledge.

Purple-crowned Woodnymph

Thalurania colombica • Male: 4 inches (10 cm), Female: 3¹/₂ inches (9 cm)

Very slight variations in color have given rise to this species, which is also known as the Violet Woodnymph and Violet-crowned Woodnymph, although subspecies found in Guatemala and Honduras *(T. c. townsendi)* and Colombia into northwest Venezuela *(T. c. colombica)* are known as the Blue-crowned Woodnymph and Colombian Woodnymph, respectively. Two other subspecies are recognized; *T. c. venusta* is found in eastern Nicaragua through Costa Rica and into central Panama, and *T. c. rostrifera* is found in the far northwest of Venezuela.

They are all thought to be sedentary, although dispersion occurs after breeding, and there is movement coinciding with food availability.

This hummingbird is more of a forest dweller, keeping to the shaded areas of humid forests and forest edges and avoiding more open habitats. However, it can be found in shrubby yards shaded by trees or on plantations and in secondary growth.

This species regularly hawks for insects in "flycatcher fashion," choosing a prominent twig below the tree canopy from which to hunt. It will also glean among the foliage for insects and spiders. Nectar is taken from a broad range of flowering plants, in particular small shrubs and trees as well as epiphytes, but seldom from outside the tree canopy.

Males are purple-violet on their forehead, crown, and belly, with patches of similar coloration at the bend of the wing and across the upper

back. The deeply forked tail is also dark violet. The nape, lower back, and rump are a bronze-green, sometimes tinged violet; the wings are black with a bluish sheen, and the throat and upper breast are iridescent bright green. The straight bill is black. Females are bright green, including the upperparts, wing coverts, and the flanks extending into the belly. The remainder of the underparts are gray-buff, becoming darker in the center of the belly. Her almost straight-cut tail is bronze-green at the coverts, becoming blue-black at the end, and the three outer tail feathers have white tips.

It chooses the drier weather in which to breed. The small, cup-shaped nest is usually placed low down on top of a branch and hidden beneath a large leaf. Plant down and spiderwebs intermixed with pieces of tree fern, moss, and lichen are used in its construction. No other reliable information is available on breeding.

Fork-tailed Woodnymph

Thalurania furcata • 3–4 inches (7¹/₂–10 cm)

This mainly sedentary species is widely distributed throughout most of South America, north of the Tropic of Capricorn and east of the Andes, apart from the northeastern coast of Brazil. At present most of the thirteen recognized subspecies are fairly common, but deforestation in many areas is giving cause for concern. It is found in a wide range of habitats, particularly in humid forests and along forest edges. It can be found on plantations and in secondary woodland, and also in gardens and more open areas. Its favorite sources of nectar include the flowers of many trees and shrubs as well as vines, epiphytes, and large herbs such as heliconia. It also gleans for insects and spiders and hawks for small flies.

Males of this species all have dark, dull green upperparts, with a brown-green nape and crown. The underparts are dark blue, sometimes tinged violet, as is the narrow collar band across the upper back. The throat and face are an iridescent bright green. The forked tail is blackish-blue with dark gray-blue undertail coverts showing whiter edges. The lower belly and vent are gray, but in one subspecies, *T. f. balzani*, the vent and undertail coverts appear almost all white. The flight feathers are black with bronze-green wing coverts and a violet-blue patch on the bend of the wing. The straight bill is black and varies slightly in length among the subspecies. Females have slightly brighter green upperparts that are tinged with a dull brown on the crown. Underparts are a dull buff-gray, and the tail feathers blue-black with the three outer feathers tipped white. The various subspecies are individually recognized by slight variations in plumage coloration but are all about the same size, apart from *T. f. furcatoides* from the lower Amazon region of eastern Brazil, which is slightly larger. As would be expected, there is intermixing of the subspecies where they meet at their boundaries, and plumages take on traits from each subspecies.

It is thought that breeding takes place from April to October. No other reliable information is available on breeding.

White-chinned Sapphire

Hylocharis cyanus • 3-3½ inches (7½–9 cm)

The five subspecies of the White-chinned Sapphire are widespread in their distribution, preferring forest edges and damp woodland to the arid regions. They are more of a lowland species, found in some places at the coast but more often at slightly higher elevations from 600 feet to just over 3,000 feet above sea level. The nominate subspecies, *H. c. cyanus*, is resident along the eastern coast of Brazil from Pernambuco to São Paulo, where it intermixes with *H. c. griseiventris,* which ranges further south to Buenos Aires in Argentina. *H. c. viridiventris* extends its range from northern Colombia eastward through the Guianas and into northern Brazil. *H. c. conversa* is found in a broad strip that covers eastern Bolivia through northern Paraguay and into southwestern Brazil, and *H. c. rostrata* covers a large area of the Amazonas. It is quite often found close to human habitation and readily accepts secondary growth, clearings, plantations, parks, and gardens, as well as open areas with scattered trees. It is a nectar feeder but also eats numerous insects and spiders, which it gleans from foliage.

Upperparts are a brilliant iridescent yellow-green, which blend into a bronze-red at the rump. The tail is blue-black. The forehead and cheeks leading down to the neck and around to the lower throat are a bright violet-blue. Below this, the underparts are gray-green at the center of the belly and become greener at the lower belly and flanks. The chin and upper throat are white to off-white. The straight bill is red with a black tip in the male, although some have darker upper mandibles. The female is similar but lacks the violet-blue coloring on the head. She has slightly brighter green coloration, with an all-green forehead, crown, and ear coverts. Her underparts are greenish with patches of buff-gray to white in the center of the belly, throat, and undertail coverts.

Breeding takes place at almost any time of the year. A cup-shaped nest is built on top of a branch anywhere up to about ten feet above the ground. The construction is mainly of plant fibers interlaced with spiderwebs and decorated with small pieces of lichen. The female incubates her two eggs for two weeks, and the young fledge some three to four weeks later.

Rufous-tailed Hummingbird

Amazilia tzacatl • 3$\frac{1}{4}$-4$\frac{1}{2}$ inches (8-11 cm)

This little hummingbird is also known as the Rieffer's or the Escudo Hummingbird, and there are four subspecies. The nominate subspecies, *A. t. tzacatl*, is found from the central and eastern side of Mexico southeastward to central Panama. *A. t. handleyi* is the largest and inhabits the island of Escudo de Veraguas off northwest Panama. The range of *A. t. fuscicaudata* covers western Venezuela through north to western Colombia, and *A. t. jucunda* covers southwest Colombia through western Ecuador.

Throughout the range, it is found in a huge variety of habitats, from beaches and mangrove on the coast to open forests 8,000 feet up in the Andes. It seems to prefer clearings and forest edges, whether they are cultivated plantations or evergreen forests, but is seldom seen in dense growth. It feeds from ground level to the tree canopy, often hanging on adjacent foliage or petals to get at flower nectar. It also gleans for spiders and insects along the surface of branches and among leafy foliage. Like many other hummingbirds, it makes use of the holes pierced into the base of flowers by the Bananaquit (*Coereba flaveola*) to reach the nectar. Where the availability of its food sources is relatively stable, the birds are more sedentary, but in the drier hilly areas, there is likely to be some altitudinal migration as food becomes scarce.

Upperparts and upper belly vary from a metallic bronze-green to a golden-green, with iridescence creating colors of turquoise-blue and yellow mainly on the throat. The lower belly varies from pale gray to brown-gray. The tail is a pale chestnut. The female is similar to the

male, differing mainly at the throat, where the plumage appears more mottled, and at the belly, which is white. The red bill usually has a black tip, but the upper mandible can sometimes show black throughout.

Breeding can take place at almost any time of the year, but there are regional variations. The nest is more likely to be built on a horizontal branch six to twelve feet above the ground, but other sites are occasionally chosen. Plant fibers are formed into a cup shape and bound together with spiderwebs before being decorated with lichens and pieces of dead leaf. The female incubates her two eggs for just over two weeks, and the young fledge around three weeks later.

Amazilia Hummingbird

Amazilia amazilia • 3^1/$_2$-4^1/$_2$ inches (9–11 cm)

Four subspecies of the Amazilia Hummingbird are recognized. The bird shown here is the Dumerill's Hummingbird *(Amazilia amazilia dumerilii)*, which lives west of the Andes, from northern Peru through western Ecuador as well as in areas of southeast Ecuador. The other three subspecies are found west of the Andes in Peru. Quite common in cultivated areas and yards and often observed in towns and cities, it can also be located in more natural habitats of open dry desert areas with scattered scrub and thorn forests from submontane regions and right down to the coast. It is also occasionally seen in forested areas. It is generally thought to be resident, but there is often a dispersal to different altitudes after breeding. Besides feeding on nectar, it will also forage for small insects and spiders.

This species has dark to yellow-green upperparts that blend into rufous tail feathers on the lower back. The red bill is straight with a dark, almost black tip; the dark area on the lower mandible often extends halfway along the bill. The throat is a mottled dark turquoise-green. The breast and belly are light chestnut-brown, becoming very pale at the vent. Females are similar, but often have paler underparts, particularly on the lower belly. The subspecies *A. a. dumerilii* and *A. a. leucophaea* have a few white chin markings and patches of white below the green throat and on the belly.

Breeding can take place at almost any time of the year. A cup-shaped nest of fine plant fibers bound together with spiderwebs is constructed on the top of a flat horizontal branch. Nests can also be located in dense bushes for protection where adverse wet weather conditions persist. Two eggs are incubated by the female for up to eighteen days. Fledging takes place after another three weeks.

Cinnamon Hummingbird

Amazilia rutila • 4 inches (10 cm)

The nominate subspecies of the Cinnamon Hummingbird, *A. r. rutila*, is found in the southwestern coastal states of Mexico, from Oaxaca to Jalisco. *A. r. diluta* ranges northward through Nayarit and Sinaloa, and *A. r. graysoni* is confined to the islands Las Tres Marias, just off Nayarit. The fourth subspecies, *A. r. corallirostris*, extends from the Yucatán in Mexico down into Chiapas, and then along the Pacific coast through much of Guatemala, Honduras, and Nicaragua and into Costa Rica. Although it prefers the drier tropical habitat, the Cinnamon Hummingbird can be found in a wide variety of environments and especially more open forest. It is common at lower elevations, especially in areas of secondary growth, and is often found close to human habitation. Its main diet is nectar from flowering trees and shrubs, as well as from vines and other plants. Insects and spiders are also eaten, and flies are often caught by hawking.

The cinnamon-rufous underparts are evident both in males and females of all subspecies, although there is some variation in color density. Most show a pale to white patch at the vent. The upperparts are bright green over the head and bends of the wing, becoming golden-bronze over the back. The very slightly notched tail is rufous at the base, with green-bronze to purple tips. The flight feathers are black and the male's straight bill is pinkish-red with a black tip. The female, which generally has slightly paler underparts and a brownish chin, has a mainly black bill with red at the base of the lower mandible.

Breeding can take place throughout the year, when a cup-shaped nest of fine plant fibers held together with spiderwebs and decorated with tree fern is built on a branch in a secluded shrub or low tree. Two eggs are incubated by the female for a little over two weeks.

Violet-crowned Hummingbird

Agyrtria violiceps • 4 inches (10 cm)

Often called the Azurecrown and once known as the Salvin's Hummingbird, this species was previously grouped with the *Amazilia* genus of hummingbirds and given the scientific name of *Amazilia verticalis*. Two subspecies are now recognized; the nominate, *A. v. violiceps*, inhabits southwest Mexico whereas *A. v. ellioti* ranges from central Mexico northward into the southwestern United States. As they are partial migrants, it is not unusual for them to wander into the western United States to southeast Arizona and southern California.

This hummingbird is common throughout its range but is more often found in the south. Dry open scrubland with sycamore and agaves is a regular habitat, as are more open woodlands and forest edges of pine and oak, but they frequently come close to human habitation and into parks and yards. Birds migrating into the United States are often found in canyons where there is water and lush vegetation. They take nectar from flowering trees and tall plants, and have a particular liking for the agave. Insects and spiders are either hawked in the air or gleaned from high in the treetops.

A medium-sized hummingbird, the male is usually recognized by its gleaming all-white underparts and violet-blue crown, nape, and forehead. The upperparts and flanks are a bronze-tinged olive-green, becoming more purple on the upper tail coverts and central tail feathers. The straight bill is red tipped with black. Females are similar, but with the nape and the back of the neck tinged turquoise.

Breeding is usually from April to August, with nests being built high in trees in the north of the range but often lower down in the south. The cup-shaped nest is constructed of plant fibers and down intermixed with lichens and bound together with spiderwebs on top of a horizontal branch. The female incubates her two eggs for about two weeks; the young fledge about three weeks later.

Steely-vented Hummingbird

Saucerrottei saucerrottei • 4¹/₄ inches (11 cm)

Also known as the Blue-vented Hummingbird and the Saucerotte's Hummingbird, this species was once grouped with the *Amazilia* genus. Four subspecies are now recognized. *S. s. saucerrottei* ranges through the drier lowland areas of north and west Colombia. The western Venezuelan subspecies, *S. s. braccata*, keeps more to the foothills at around 6,500 feet. *S. s. warscewiczi* is also found in the far north of Colombia but extends its range just into Venezuela. *S. s. hoffmanni* is isolated in the south and southwest of Nicaragua and the western half of Costa Rica.

This species keeps mainly to the lowlands and foothills, preferring more open habitats such as savannas and open dry forest with shrubby exuberances. Areas of scrub, forest edges, and, frequently, yards and gardens are exploited for nectar from flowering trees and shrubs. Epiphytes and vines are also used, along with many of the low-growing plants. Spiders and insects are often gleaned from foliage.

Although at first it appears to be one of the more mundane-colored hummingbirds, the general overall green appearance of this bird has outstanding iridescence, particularly on the breast in certain light. The male's slightly forked tail is blue-black, as are the upper tail coverts. The undertail coverts are a steely blue, often tinged green. He has a straight bill; the upper mandible is black and the lower mandible is orange-red with a black tip. The female has a similar appearance, but shows white mottling on the throat and brownish undertail coverts. Her tail is notched rather than forked.

There seems to be no particular breeding season for this species, with nests being found throughout the year. A typical nest site is on the top of a horizontal branch well off the ground in a small tree. Cup-shaped nests are constructed of fine plant fibers and spiderwebs and camouflaged externally with pieces of lichen. It is known that the female incubates two eggs and they hatch in about two weeks, but no other reliable breeding information is available.

Snowcap

Microchera albocoronata • 2¹/₂ inches (6¹/₂ cm)

This tiny hummingbird is also known as the White-crowned Hummingbird, and two subspecies are recognized. The nominate and darker-colored subspecies, *M. a. albocoronata*, is found on the lower hillsides of western and central Panama. *M. a. parvirostris* ranges well to the west along a northern hillside coastal belt from western Panama through Costa Rica and Nicaragua and just into southeastern Honduras. Although it prefers natural wet forests and forest boundaries, where it exploits flowering trees and shrubs, it often ventures out into nearby hedgerows to search for small flowers, and also to glean insects and spiders. It can often be seen along forest edges hawking for aerial insects.

Easily recognized within its range by its brilliant white crown, the male has bright iridescent purple-red upperparts that become more bronze-colored on the central tail feathers. The undertail coverts are white and the outer tail feathers are whitish at the base, becoming darker toward the black tips. The underparts are blackish with a bright violet sheen over the breast, becoming bronze to green at the throat. The short, straight bill is black. Females retain the snowy-white cap, although it is smaller than the male's. They have gleaming green upperparts and gray-white underparts. The rump and tail appear reddish-bronze; the tail has a darker subterminal band.

Nests are usually constructed on top of a low branch from very fine plant fibers and pieces of tree fern bound together with spiderwebs and decorated with moss and lichen. No reliable information is available on breeding.

Blue-throated Hummingbird

Lampornis clemenciae • 5 inches (13 cm)

This species is regularly found in the far southwestern United States and into Mexico, usually in mountain ranges at altitudes above 5,000 feet. *L. c. clemenciae* ranges into southwest Texas southward through the center of Mexico as far as Oaxaca. *L. c. bessophilus* has a more northwesterly distribution and is found in a band from the south of Arizona and southwest New Mexico southward through western Chihuahua and eastern Sonora. It is a bird of the drier mountain slopes and canyons, and is often found in riverine habitats with a plentiful growth of low flowering plants from which it can obtain nectar. It also eats a wide variety of insects and spiders. Artificial feeding, particularly in the United States, has encouraged unnaturally large congregations that could not be supported by natural means. As a medium-sized hummingbird, it does exert a certain amount of dominance over other hummingbirds at feeding stations. There is some altitudinal migration of birds in the south of the range, and many of the more northerly birds migrate south for the winter.

The male has an attractive iridescent bright blue gorget that contrasts with buffish-gray underparts and brown-gray ear coverts. The ear coverts are bordered to the rear by a broad white stripe and there is often a short, thin, mustachelike white stripe. The upperparts are bronze-green, with lighter green across the top of the back. Bronze-colored tail coverts overlay a blackish-blue rounded tail, tipped white on the outer feathers. The wings and slightly decurved bill are black. Females are a little duller and look almost identical, but have buffish-gray underparts, including the throat.

The breeding season is geared to flowering seasons, and in the United States, this occurs from May to early summer. Sites are chosen for protection from above, such as thick foliage or a rock above a crevice. The nest, a cup-shaped structure, is built from fine plant fibers, moss, and lichens and is held together with spiderwebs. The outside is often decorated with pieces of lichen, twig, and bark fragments. The female incubates her two eggs for two and a half weeks; the young fledge almost a month later.

Variable Mountain-gem

Lampornis castaneoventris • 4¹/₂ inches (11¹/₂ cm)

Opposite: A male Purple-throated Mountain-gem (*L. c. calolaemus*).

Below: A female Purple-throated Mountain-gem (*L. c. calolaemus*).

As might be expected for a bird with the name "Variable," there are several different forms of this species, all recognized as different subspecies, but there is debate as to whether they should be classed as different species. They are all found in a relatively small area from southern Nicaragua through Costa Rica and into western Panama, where they inhabit mainly treetops and woodland edges of mountain forests. In more open habitats, they keep to shrubby areas and may also be found on plantations and farmland. They feed on nectar from a wide variety of flowering plants; the males seem to prefer flowers of epiphytes within the forest canopy, whereas females feed lower down on flowering shrubs. Numerous insects and spiders are also taken by gleaning through foliage.

The males of the five subspecies are recognized mainly through the color of the iridescent gorget and tail. The nominate subspecies, the White-throated Mountain-gem (*L. c. castaneoventris*) of western Panama,

has a brilliant white gorget and blue-black tail, glittering bronze-green upperparts and upper breast, and the belly and vent are buffish-gray. Very similar is the Gray-tailed Mountain-gem (*L. c. cinereicauda*) from southern Costa Rica, which has a brown-gray tail, turquoise-blue forehead, and more widespread green on the breast. The Purple-throated Mountain-gem (*L. c. calolaemus*) from Costa Rica is similar to *L. c. cinereicauda* but has a purple gorget and dark blue tail. *L. c. pectoralis*, also similar, has a purple-blue gorget, turquoise-blue forehead, and glittering dark green underparts. The ear coverts are black to dark green bordered at the rear by a white stripe that leads from the rear and top of the eye down to the neck. The straight bill is all black, and the feet are reddish-brown. Females of all subspecies are similar, with green upperparts and cinnamon-red underparts. The tail is bronze-green with a blackish subterminal band and a white tip to the outer tail feathers.

This species breeds during the rainy season, selecting a low site on a branch at the edge of a clearing on which to build its cup-shaped nest. Fine plant fibers and down, along with pieces of tree fern, are bound together with spiderwebs and then decorated externally with lichens and moss. The female incubates her two eggs for between two and three weeks, and the young fledge almost a month later.

White-eared Hummingbird

Basilinna leucotis • 4 inches (10 cm)

This highland species consists of three subspecies: *B. l. pygmaea*, which ranges from southern Nicaragua through Honduras, eastern Guatemala, and north into El Salvador; *B. l. leucotis*, the nominate, extends through Guatemala northward into central Mexico; and *B. l. borealis* is found in northern Mexico. The northern subspecies has a tendency to migrate northward in the spring, and is occasionally found in southern Arizona and Texas. Highland pine-oak and pine-evergreen forests are its favorite habitats, particularly where there is an understory of flowering shrubby growth. It feeds on nectar but also hawks and gleans for insects and spiders.

The male's upperparts are mainly green, with a rufous tinge on the nape, lower back, and upper tail coverts. The forehead, crown, and chin are iridescent violet and the frontal ear coverts black, contrasting with a white stripe extending from above and behind the eye down to the neck. Immediately below the chin, the iridescent green of the gorget extends downward, blending into a grayish-green lower belly and vent. The slightly forked tail is green with the outer feathers edged black, and the straight bill is red at the base with a black tip. The female has similarly colored ear coverts and upperparts, but she lacks the violet coloration on the head. She has an all-black upper mandible and a bronze forehead and crown. The underparts are off-white, marked with iridescent green spots. Her greenish tail has bronze edges to the outer tail feathers, with white tips.

This species probably nests throughout the year. The cup-shaped nest is usually on a branch, sometimes on the top of an old nest, and is constructed from plant fibers and leaf fragments decorated with lichen. Two eggs are incubated by the female for just over two weeks, and fledging can take another four weeks.

Fawn-breasted Brilliant

Heliodoxa rubinoides • 5 inches (13 cm)

This species has several other common names, including the Lilac-breasted Brilliant, Lilac-throated Hummingbird, and Penny-throated Hummingbird. Found on the slopes of the Andes through Colombia, Ecuador, and Peru, this hummingbird is separated into three subspecies. The nominate subspecies, *H. r. rubinoides*, resides in the central and eastern Andes of Colombia. To the west of the Andes through Colombia and Ecuador, *H. r. aequatorialis* can be found, and back on the east of the Andes through Ecuador and into Peru is *H. r. cervinigularis*. Nowhere is it common, as it keps mainly to altitudes of 5,500–6,000 feet, except after breeding, when it may disperse to both higher and lower altitudes. It inhabits wet and humid forests, particularly at the edges, and often wanders further afield into agricultural and urban environments. Although it is often seen hawking for aerial insects, its main diet is nectar from flowering trees and shrubs.

The upperparts are a very dark iridescent bronze-green with blackish-bronze wings and brown-tinged wing coverts. The underparts are warm brown, becoming dark green at the flanks. The male of the nominate subspecies has a dark green throat with a small iridescent purple patch just below. The male of the subspecies *H. r. cervinigularis* has a smaller and less dense iridescent throat patch.

Breeding takes place in the latter quarter of the year in Ecuador, and in the first few months of the year in Colombia. Apart from the fact that the female incubates two eggs, no other breeding details are available.

Green-crowned Brilliant

Heliodoxa jacula • Male: 5 inches (13 cm), Female: 4¹/₂ inches (11¹/₂ cm)

Also known as the Green-fronted Brilliant, there are three subspecies. *H. j. jacula*, the nominate, is found in central and northern Colombia as far west as its border with Panama. In the far southwest of Colombia and into western Ecuador, *H. j. jamesoni* is resident. *H. j. henryi* can be located in Costa Rica and western Panama, where it undertakes an altitudinal migration down into the lowlands after breeding. The preferred habitat seems to be in the wet areas of cloud forests on the foothills and mountains that border more open countryside. Here they are found in the understory, where they search for the long, bell-shaped flowers to which they are well adapted. They are also attracted to the flowers of shrubs, especially heliconia, as well as the flowering epiphytes. This hummingbird not only hovers to feed but frequently takes the easy way out and perches on the plant itself. It will also glean foliage for spiders and insects, in addition to hawking.

The dark color of this hummingbird transforms in bright light when, in the males, the dark blue-green becomes dazzlingly brilliant. This color predominates over the head and down the throat and upper breast, apart from the white spot behind the eye and a tiny patch of iridescent violet-blue between the lower neck and breast. The lores and a very small triangular patch above the base of the bill can both appear black at times.

The upperparts from the back downward are tinged bronze, including the central tail feathers. The outer feathers of the deeply forked tail are bluish-black. The female is not as brilliant, having whitish underparts spotted green, outer tail feathers tipped white, and a whitish malar stripe. The subspecies differ slightly in plumage: the male *H. j. jamesoni* is less brilliant generally and has a short, greenish tail, whereas the male *H. j. henryi* is brighter, with a totally blue-black tail.

To date, there is little breeding information available for this species.

Magnificent Hummingbird

Eugenes fulgens • 4¹/₂–5 inches (11–13 cm)

This species is known by several other common names, in particular the Rivoli's Hummingbird. It is also called the Admiral Hummingbird, but the subspecies *E. f. spectablis*, which is found in Costa Rica and Panama, accounts for the names of Costa Rica and Panama Hummingbird. The nominate subspecies, *E. f. fulgens*, is found in the very southwest of the United States through Mexico and Central America and into northeast Nicaragua. Although the Central American populations are considered to be sedentary, there is thought to be movement of some north Mexican birds into the United States for the breeding season. It is primarily a bird of the hills but is seldom found above 8,000 feet and usually only migrates to below 5,000 feet when the weather turns cold.

It subsists on the nectar of flowering plants as well as small flies, beetles, and spiders.

Males have very dark green upperparts. The green underparts become almost black on the lower belly. The gorget is iridescent green and the crown iridescent purple. There is a dark green-black eyestripe that accentuates the small white spot behind the eye. The birds have robust, straight black bills and a bronze-colored tail. The female's plumage is more mundane, lacking iridescence on the gorget and the purple crown. Her upperparts are dark green and the underparts are grayish-buff, with the wings and tail appearing more bronze-green.

Resident birds in Central America have a breeding season that extends from November to July, but others delay the start of breeding until May. Detailed information on nesting is limited, but nests are usually found well off the ground on high tree branches. They are cup-shaped constructions of fine plant fibers lined with plant down and covered externally with pieces of lichen and tiny shreds of bark. The female incubates her two eggs for over two weeks.

Shining Sunbeam

Aglaeactis cupripennis • 4³/₄–5 inches (12–13 cm)

Also known as the Copper-winged Hummingbird, there are two recognized subspecies; the nominate, *A. c. cupripennis*, is found in the northern Andes from Colombia to central Peru. The other, *A. c. caumatonotus*, also in Peru, is seen to the south almost as far as Lake Titicaca. This species prefers the more open páramo, an area that is predominantly grassland with scattered trees and shrubs, as well as the drier mountain ridges, slopes, and cloud forests, usually where trees are present and normally above 8,000 feet. It is a resident species, although it will descend to lower elevations in inclement weather.

Although it takes aerial insects by hawking, its main diet consists of nectar from flowering vines, shrubs, trees, and bromeliads.

The Shining Sunbeam is by far the most widely distributed and is fairly common throughout its range, whereas the other Sunbeam hummingbirds have restricted ranges. Although of similar plumage to the others of the *Agleactis* genus, being characterized by their brilliant iridescent lower back and rump on an otherwise mundane-colored plumage, it has much lighter rufous-brown underparts. Their iridescent back patch is almost rainbow-colored, contrasting with dark brown wings, mantle, and crown. The tail is also dark brown, becoming rufous at the lower tail coverts. The short, straight bill is black. Females are similar, but the iridescent back patch is either less bright or is replaced by brown.

It is known to nest at all times of the year depending on location. It usually chooses a site high in a tree, often attaching its nest to an epiphyte. Mosses, lichens, plant fibers, and hairs are bound together to form a cup-shaped nest, which is decorated externally with small pieces of lichen, leaves, and bark. Two eggs are laid, taking around eighteen days to incubate. It is almost four weeks before the young fledge.

Collared Inca

Coeligena torquata • 5³/₄ inches (14¹/₂ cm)

Also known as the White-cravat Hummingbird, it is easy to see why. All six subspecies of this large hummingbird, both males and females, sport an immaculate broad white collar. They are all fairly sedentary inhabitants of edges and clearings of humid montane forests in the Andes. The nominate subspecies, *C. t. torquata*, ranges from northern Peru and eastern Ecuador up through Colombia and eastward into western Venezuela. *C. t. eisenmanni* is from southern Peru, *C. t. insectivora* from central Peru, and *C. t. margaretae* from northern Peru. Farther north in Ecuador, *C. t. fulgidigula* is found to the west of the Andes, and in northwest Venezuela in the Andes south of Lake Maracaibo is *C. t. conradii*. They keep below the canopy, searching for nectar from flowering trees and shrubs. Insects and spiders are gleaned from foliage, and flies are caught by hawking.

All subspecies have mostly iridescent green upperparts, bellies, and central tail feathers; the color varies in darkness among subspecies. The outer tail feathers of the forked tail are white at the base, with shining green tips. Apart from *C. t. conradii*, which has a green head, males have black foreheads and napes and green chins. The nominate subspecies and males of *C. t. fulgidigula* have purplish-blue crown spots, and all have small white spots behind the eye. They have long and straight black bills. Females lack the green chins and instead have a dirty white plumage that is sometimes tinged buffish-orange and spotted with green.

Although breeding information is scant, nests have been found on cliff faces, hidden among ferns. The cup-shaped nest is built mainly from plant fibers and fern pieces. As with most hummingbird species, the two eggs are incubated only by the female.

Sword-billed Hummingbird

Ensifera ensifera • 6³/₄–9 inches (17–23 cm)

This hummingbird deserves its name, as its black, slightly upturned bill, shaped like a sword, has a length of around four inches, about half the bird's overall length and certainly the longest bill of any hummingbird. Although its bill looks like an overgrown appendage that may put it to a disadvantage, the Sword-billed Hummingbird is well adapted to feeding from long, pendulous flower blooms. Its unusual appearance has also been instrumental in its gaining notoriety—and thereby protection—by being listed as an attraction to many of the protected areas and national parks of Peru, Bolivia, Ecuador, and Colombia. It is a sedentary species ranging through the Andes from western Venezuela in the north to northern Bolivia, where it prefers high mountain forests, especially forest edges.

Not only does it feed by hovering below flowers, it will often perch or hang on to flowers from below in order to probe upward for nectar. It also hawks for insects, looking very ungainly as it darts about with its huge bill wide open.

The male has dark green upperparts and underparts, with a reddish tinge on the head, and black on the chin and throat. The underparts often

appear iridescent and grayish on the lower belly. The forked tail and long wings are greenish-black. It has a small white spot behind the eye. Females are similar but duller, with a less-forked tail and pale-edged outer tail feathers. Her underparts are grayish-buff with darker green spots.

Little is known of its breeding habits, likely due to inaccessible nest sites high in the tree canopy.

Giant Hummingbird

Patagona gigas • 7³/₄-8³/₄ inches (20-22 cm)

Compared to the Bee Hummingbird, this is literally a giant and without doubt the largest of the hummingbird family.

Two subspecies are recognized. *P. g. gigas* breeds in Chile and western Argentina and migrates across the Andes into northwest Argentina in the fall. The more northern subspecies, *P. g. peruviana*, is found in the Andes from southwest Colombia through Ecuador, Peru, and Bolivia to the Atacama Desert in northern Chile. Its preferred habitat is dry and open with shrubs, cacti, and scattered small trees, but in some places, it frequents riverside vegetation and hedgerows close to human habitation.

Males are recognized by a conspicuous white rump accentuated against dull olive-brown upperparts and cinnamon-colored underparts and sides of the neck. The upper tail coverts and feathers surrounding the

rump have distinctive white edges. Females can be similar to males but are generally duller with more spotted underparts. All have a substantial straight black bill and brownish-green forked tails.

It can weigh up to twenty-three grams, but the norm is about nineteen grams. Not only does it hover with a wing beat that is slower than normal for hummingbirds, it frequently flies and glides in a swiftlike manner. It is less likely to hover than most hummingbirds and often feeds while perched.

Its diet is primarily flower nectar, but it also consumes numerous insects, which it hawks from a perch or snatches while hovering among a swarm. A favorite flower seems to be the agave, a tropical fleshy-leafed plant that has very tall, flowering stalks and from which sisal is obtained. This plant is thought to have been introduced to Ecuador and northern Peru in the sixteenth century and is probably the reason for a northward expansion of the species range. Other common food sources are the flowers of several tall cacti as well as many different shrubs, providing a succession of nectar sources within its established territory.

Although very territorial and of an aggressive nature, it can be seen feeding in small groups where food sources are particularly abundant.

Its breeding season depends on its location. In Peru, this extends from September for six or seven months. In Chile, it is later and shorter—from October to January. In Ecuador it is later still, from December to March. The nest is made from moss and lichen bound together with spiderwebs and lined with hair, wool, or soft fine plant fibers. It is usually situated on a branch of a tree, but occasionally on a cactus. Two eggs are usually laid, taking just under two weeks to hatch.

Green-backed Firecrown

Sephanoides sephanoides • 4¼ inches (10½ cm)

The breeding range of this species is from Tierra del Fuego in
Argentina and across and up into the foothills of the Andes of Chile
and Argentina as far as the Atacama Desert. Birds from the south of the
range move northward to winter mainly in central Argentina. It is quite
common and can be found on the coast and into the foothills up to an
elevation of around 6,500 feet. Not only does it like the wilder habitat of
forest clearings and edges, where it congregates in substantial numbers
around flowering trees, but it also frequents urban parkland and yards.
It takes mainly nectar from flowering trees, shrubs, and other plants,
supplemented occasionally with insects gleaned from foliage.

Both the male and female have bronze-green upperparts; the male
has an iridescent yellow-red crown and forehead. The slightly forked
tail and the wings are also bronze-green. The underparts are buffish-
white densely scattered with iridescent green and brownish spots. The
density of spots increases at the flanks, giving a suffused green-bronze
appearance. There is a small white spot to the rear of the eye, and the
short, straight bill is black.

Breeding takes place during the latter quarter of the year, but few
details of breeding are available. Tiny, cup-shaped nests of plant fibers
and spiderwebs are attached to branches, often overhanging water, and
two eggs are laid.

Juan Fernandez Firecrown

Sephanoides fernandenis • 4³/₄ inches (12 cm)

Also called the Fernandez Firecrown, this species is highly endangered, with only a few hundred birds known to exist on Robinson Crusoe Island off the west coast of Chile. Its decline is attributed to habitat erosion caused by human incursion into the Juan Fernandez group of islands. Destruction of habitat due to logging as well as from the introduced goats and rabbits, together with the smothering effects on regenerating plants caused by introduced bramble, are all thought to be causes for the species' decline. Although it seems to prefer shaded and more secluded habitats of forests and dense pockets of woodland, it is often found near human habitation and even within towns when attracted by flowering trees. Well adapted to the many species of plants found in the region, it is particularly attracted to the Juan Fernandez cabbage tree (*Dendroseris littoralis*). It seeks out nectar from flowers of many plants, but seldom in the bright sunshine and often well above the ground.

This is one of the few hummingbirds with striking sexual dimorphism. The male is easily recognized by his dark orange plumage, brown-gray wings, and iridescent fiery orange-yellow crown. The short bill is black. The very different female has yellow-green upperparts that become bluish on the rump. The crown is iridescent purple-blue, the tail is blue-green with the outer feathers having white inner webs, and the underparts are white with spotted iridescent green over the throat and flanks.

No reliable breeding information is available.

Greenish Puffleg

Haplophaedia aureliae • 3¹/₂–4 inches (9–10 cm)

The three subspecies of the Greenish Puffleg are all from separate areas of the Andes in the far northwest of South America. Although mainly sedentary, some are forced to move to lower altitudes during severe weather. The nominate subspecies, *H. a. aureliae*, is found on the eastern side of the Andes from Colombia southward just into Ecuador. *H. a. caucensis* keeps to the central and western Andes of Colombia, extending northward and into the far east of Panama, whereas *H. a. russata* is found in the eastern Andes of Ecuador.

All prefer the montane and submontane humid and wet forests, where they feed on flowering trees and shrubs below the tree canopy. They also eat insects that they glean from the foliage. They establish feeding territories that are vigorously defended, driving off any other birds that dare to approach.

All three subspecies are similar in appearance, having iridescent green upperparts tinged reddish, with the top of the head and ear coverts a coppery-red. Underparts are dull green with very visible white leg puffs. The rump is reddish-bronze, and the slightly notched tail bluish-black. Between the subspecies, variations occur mainly on the breast and rump, although the Ecuadorian subspecies has a slightly longer bill. Its underparts are dull brownish-green and upperparts a bright copper-red, especially at the rump. *H. a. caucensis* has a patch of white on the lower belly and appears to have brighter green upperparts. All have straight black bills and a small white spot to the rear of the eye.

Breeding generally takes place between December and March, when a nest site is chosen, well protected from inclement weather. The cup-shaped nest, often low down under heliconia leaves, is constructed mainly of mosses with a few plant fibers and spiderwebs. Two eggs are incubated by the female and take just over two weeks to hatch.

Booted Racquet-tail

Ocreatus underwoodii • 6 inches (15 cm)

Also called the Racquet-tail or Racquet-tailed Hummingbird, this is a common species in the montane forests of the Andes, from northern Venezuela to Bolivia in the south. There are as many as eight subspecies, with considerable differences between them. The nominate subspecies, *O. u. underwoodii*, is found in the eastern Andes of Colombia and has both upperparts and underparts of iridescent green, although the forehead is more bronze-green. The male's deeply forked tail is green at the shorter inner feathers and grayer toward the outer feathers, which are substantially elongated at the tips, extending into long black shafts with blue-black racquets at the ends. He has brownish-green ear coverts and a small white spot behind the eye. His legs and feet are almost hidden by large white leg puffs and his short, straight bill is black. The female's upperparts are similar, although the rump is occasionally finely spotted with buff. She has a short, deeply forked green tail with bluish outer feathers tipped white. Her underparts are white medially and are heavily spotted with iridescent green at the flanks. Her white leg puffs are smaller than the male's.

The male *O. u. melanantherus* from Ecuador is similar to the nominate subspecies, but has a black chin and bluish tips to the tail feathers. The female has more white and is less spotted on the underparts. The southern subspecies, *O. u. addae, annae*, and *peruanus*, all have rufous leg puffs. The more northern subspecies, *O. u. polysticus* and *discifer*, have bronzer upperparts, whereas *O. u. incommodus* from the west and central Andes of Colombia has a patch of black over the chin and throat. All subspecies are adaptable to more open secondary forests as well as wet forests. They take nectar from flowering trees, shrubs, and bromeliads, and hawk for insects.

There seems to be no particular breeding season. The small, neat, cup-shaped constructions are built with plant fibers and pieces of lichen on top of a thin branch. The female incubates two eggs for two and a half weeks, and the young fledge about three weeks later.

Red-tailed Comet

Sappho sparganura • Male: 8 inches (20 cm), Female: 5 inches (13 cm)

The nominate subspecies of this beautiful, long-tailed hummingbird, *S. s. sparganura*, is spread through the arid Andes mountain slopes of northern and central Bolivia. The more orange-colored southerly subspecies, *S. s. sappho*, has a range that extends from southwestern Bolivia through western Argentina almost as far as the Callaqui and Villarica volcanoes. It has a local altitudinal migration, going up to 13,000 feet and moving down to lower elevations of around 5,000 feet during the cold winter. Its habitat varies from more open, semiarid hillsides sparsely populated with small trees and bushes to dry deciduous forests. It feeds on a broad range of flower nectar, and forages and hawks for insects.

Males are recognized by their beautifully elongated and deeply forked and iridescent red or orange-red tail, with the individual feathers broadly tipped blackish-purple. The back is red to reddish-purple, and the head, throat, and a patch on the bend of the wing are all iridescent green. The underparts are green and the flight feathers dark green to black. The short, very slightly curved bill is black. Females also have a longish tail, but it is much shorter than the male's. It is similarly colored, but the barring shown by the black feather bands is much less distinct. The longer outer tail feathers appear pale on their outside edges. She has an iridescent green head and upperparts that become purplish at the rump. The underparts are buff and heavily marked with green spots, particularly at the throat.

This species prefers to nest on cliff faces and below overhanging rocks. The nest, a substantial, cup-shaped construction of moss, hair, and lichens, is usually established on a ledge or fixed to exposed roots. Two eggs are laid and are incubated by the female for nearly three weeks. The chicks fledge a little more than three weeks later.

Blue-tufted Starthroat

Heliomaster furcifer • **5 inches (13 cm)**

This species is often found in the lowlands of the area extending from central and eastern Bolivia, taking in southern Matto Grosso to Goias and Rio Grande du Sul in Brazil, Paraguay, western Uruguay, and northern Argentina. It prefers a grassland habitat often associated with trees and forest edges. Its diet consists mainly of nectar from a wide variety of flowering plants, including trees, shrubs, cacti, herbs, and bromeliads. Aerial insects are also hawked from a prominent perch, and other insects and spiders are taken by foraging through foliage.

The male's upperparts are iridescent bronze-green with the forehead, crown, nape, and upper mantle bright blue-green. The sharp, forked tail is green; dark above with a blue sheen below. The gorget is iridescent dark blue with a patch of brilliant violet in the center of the throat, and the feathers at the sides of the neck extend backward almost to the nape. The underparts are also very dark iridescent blue, becoming green toward

the vent. The long, slightly decurved bill is black. The female is more mundanely colored, with brownish-green upperparts and a coppery-red crown and nape. The underparts are generally gray with a patch of grayish-white on the lower belly and a green tinge at the flanks. Her tail shows dark green above, becoming darker toward the tip; from below it is brilliant blue-green with white tips on the outer feathers. After breeding, the male goes into an eclipse plumage, losing his dark blue coloration and appearing similar to the female.

The breeding season is from late November to March. The nest site is often ten to twenty feet off the ground, on top of a branch. A cup-shaped nest is built of fine plant fibers interwoven with a few spiderwebs and decorated with pieces of lichen. The female incubates the two eggs for just over two weeks; the young fledge three to four weeks later.

Oasis Hummingbird

Rhodopis vesper • **5–5¹/₂ inches (13–13¹/₂ cm)**

This mainly sedentary species has three subspecies distributed along the western slopes and coastal hills bordering the Andes through Peru to the Atacama Desert in northern Chile. The nominate subspecies, *R. v. vesper*, is found from northwestern Peru southward and just into northern Chile. *R. v. atacamensis* is found within the Atacama Desert, whereas *R. v. koepckeae* is restricted to a small area in the far northwest of Peru. It lives in the arid mountainous zones below 10,000 feet down into hilly and lowland coastal areas, where it is most common.

It prefers to feed from nectar-bearing flowers of trees, shrubs, and cacti, and can therefore be found in oases—as its name implies—but it is also frequently seen close to human habitation in parks and yards. Its diet is also supplemented by insects and spiders caught by gleaning or hawking.

Males have olive-green upperparts with a bright sheen becoming chestnut at the rump and on the upper tail coverts. The deeply forked tail is dark brown, tinged purple with the central feathers a lighter color. The underparts are whitish, and become greenish at the flanks. The throat and neck are a bright iridescent violet with turquoise-blue patches below the ear coverts, and there is a white eyebrow. The long and slightly curved bill is black. Females have similar olive-green upperparts but lack the bright throat and neck coloration, having dirty white underparts. The white eyebrow is also less pronounced. She has a shorter and only slightly forked tail, which is mainly olive-green but black toward the ends of the outer feathers, with white tips. It is pale gray below.

Breeding occurs from September to November, with nests being constructed in low fruit trees among the outer branches. Cup-shaped suspended nests of plant fibers, hair, lichen, and pieces of dry leaf are held together with spiderwebs. Two eggs are incubated by the female for a little over two weeks, and the young fledge around three and a half weeks later.

Magenta-throated Woodstar

Calliphlox bryantae • 3¹/₂ inches (9 cm)

This small hummingbird enjoys the southern mountain slopes of an area extending from northern Costa Rica to western Panama. Its favorite habitat seems to be close to forest edges and in clearings. It likes open areas of grassland and pasture with a scattering of shrubs and trees, and at times large numbers can congregate in such places. It depends on nectar from flowering shrubs, trees, and plants, often very close to the ground, and it also gleans insects and spiders from foliage, as well as hawking flies from a prominent perch. The typical feeding posture, especially of the male, is to raise the forked tail high while keeping it closed.

As its name implies, the throat, or gorget, of the male is a brilliant iridescent magenta-purple. Below his gorget is a broad white band that runs right around the upper breast almost to the nape. Around the center of the breast is a glittering green band that blends into a thin band of rufous that gives way to a whitish vent. The upperparts are bronze-green, and there is a white spot behind the eye. The long and deeply forked tail is blackish-green with the short inner feathers tipped black. The inner webs of the outer feathers are reddish-brown. The black bill is short and straight. The female has bronze-green upperparts but lacks the magenta gorget of the male. She has mainly whitish underparts that are green and rufous at the flanks. The throat is buffish at the chin and white below, bordered by a pale rufous band leading up to grayish ear coverts. She has a shorter forked tail shaped like two round lobes. The inner feathers are bronze with a black subterminal band and the outer feathers are rufous, also with a black subterminal band, but the tips are pale rufous.

Breeding is thought to take place between November and April, but no reliable breeding data is currently available.

Ruby-throated Hummingbird

Archilochus colubris • 3¹/₂ inches (9 cm)

Above: A female Ruby-throated Hummingbird (*Archilochus colubris*).

Opposite: A male Ruby-throated Hummingbird (*Archilochus colubris*).

The Ruby-throated Hummingbird is the most widespread hummingbird in the United States and Canada. It is found throughout the central and eastern United States, from the Gulf Coast northward into a band across southern Canada from Nova Scotia to central Alberta. It migrates there for the breeding season from its wintering grounds in central Mexico southward into western Panama, although some remain in southern Florida. The migration path taken by most of these birds follows a route around the Gulf of Mexico. Its wintering habitat is primarily dry lowland forests and scrub, but breeding takes place more in mixed woodland habitats, including low-lying secondary forests. It is also frequently observed in more open parkland as well as domestic yards. It feeds from a wide variety of flowering plants and shrubs. A large number of insects and spiders are also consumed, especially during migration. Although insects are gleaned from foliage, this species is adept at hawking for flies.

The gorget of the male is an iridescent ruby-red bordered above by a black stripe passing from the lores and below the eye and through the ear coverts. Below is a white band blending into a grayish belly with greenish flanks. From the forehead to the rump, the upperparts are an iridescent green down to the central feathers of the forked tail. The outer tail feathers are brownish-gray. It has a small white spot behind the eye and a short, straight, dark-colored bill. The female lacks the ruby throat, having white underparts speckled gray-green at the throat and washed gray at the flanks.

The breeding season lasts from April to late July, with the male arriving in his breeding territory a few days before the females. Cup-shaped nests are constructed on top of horizontal branches from plant fibers and lichens bound together with spiderwebs and decorated externally with pieces of lichen. Two eggs are incubated by the female for just over two weeks; the young fledge after another two to three weeks.

Black-chinned Hummingbird

Archilochus alexandri • 4 inches (10 cm)

This migratory species breeds from southwestern Canada through the western United States, as far south as Baja California and northern Mexico, and eastward as far as the Gulf of Mexico. It winters in western and southern Mexico, where a number are also thought to be resident. Breeding can start as early as March in the south of its range, but occurs two to three months later farther north. A large proportion of the migrants finish their long journey south by September.

During the breeding season, they occupy woodland and scrub, often in arid regions, and also in desert scrubland with adjacent rivers, seldom going above 6,500 feet.

They rely on nectar from a succession of flowering plants and also eat small flies, which are hawked in the air.

The male's plumage is a medium iridescent green over the upperparts with white underparts becoming green at the flanks. The wings and forked tail are dark green, with the outer tail feathers appearing lighter. His chin is black, extending in a triangle back behind the eye that takes in the ear coverts. This area of black becomes iridescent violet along the bottom edge. There is a small white spot behind the eye. The longish bill is dark brown-black. Females are similar, but their chin, ear coverts, and throat are whitish with buff spots on the throat. Her tail is more rounded, with white tips on the outer three feathers. She is almost impossible to distinguish from the female Ruby-throated Hummingbird (*Archilochus colubris*).

A cup-shaped nest is constructed from a mixture of lichens, pieces of leaf and bark, and plant down held together with spiderwebs, usually situated on the top of a branch about ten feet above the ground and overhanging running water. In some areas, a large number of yellow plant fibers are worked into the nest construction. The female usually incubates her two eggs for just over two weeks, and fledging can take up to three weeks.

Anna's Hummingbird

Calypte anna • 4–4¹/₂ inches (10–11 cm)

This species is confined mainly to the western United States and Canada, with movements occurring southward into Mexico and Baja California. In recent years, it has extended its winter range to the southeast into the central area of northern Mexico and is occasionally found farther east. Its breeding range is from northwest Mexico through the western United States, taking in a large area of southern Arizona, to southwest Canada.

It is found up to 6,000 feet in a wide variety of habitats, including coastal scrub, river valleys, and woodlands—especially oaks and evergreens—and often close to human habitation in towns and cities.

Nectar from flowering plants provides a major food source, but this hummingbird also consumes quantities of small flies and spiders, which it hawks or gleans from foliage.

The upperparts of the male are a bright yellow-green and the underparts appear a dirty grayish-green. His head is masked with

Opposite: A male Anna's Hummingbird (*Calypte anna*).

Below: A female Anna's Hummingbird (*Calypte anna*).

152

iridescent red coloring reaching down to the extended feathers of the gorget. The tail is bronze-green. The shortish bill is black. Females lack the bright red head coloration, and are instead grayish, often with pink spots on the throat and a small white spot behind the eye. Her outer tail feathers have white tips.

In favorable weather conditions, breeding begins as early as November and extends through May or even July at higher altitudes. The nest site is usually on a horizontal branch or twig anywhere from six feet above the ground to the tops of tall trees. Plant fibers, animal hair, and feathers are bound together with spiderwebs to form a cup-shaped nest, which is decorated externally with small pieces of lichen, leaves, and bark. The female incubates two eggs for two to two and a half weeks. It takes another two and a half to three and a half weeks for the young to fledge.

Costa's Hummingbird

Calypte costae • 3-3¹/₂ inches (7¹/₂–8¹/₂ cm)

The Costa's Hummingbird is a partial migrant, moving south to spend the winter in the south and west of Mexico, migrating north into the western United States to breed. It reaches to the north as far as southwest Utah and southern Nevada and into central California to breed, but after breeding, some birds disperse as far north as southern Canada and to Texas in the east. Its breeding area is mainly north of central Sonora.

This is a lowland species. During the breeding season, they are found in open dry country, including coastal scrub, desert, and scrubby foothills. They seek out areas where flowering shrubs are abundant and often where a variety of trees are present. Males set up their territories in open areas. After breeding, females and young move away into lusher vegetation and are found particularly in lowland meadows, yards, and among fruit trees.

Besides being a nectar feeder, the Costa's Hummingbird consumes large quantities of insects and spiders. It will glean among shrubs and plant foliage and also hawk for aerial insects as they swarm.

The attractive plumage of the male is accentuated by its brilliantly colored mask. Both the crown and gorget of elongated plumes are a dark iridescent violet that stands out from the dull bronze-green upperparts. The upper breast is white, extending beneath the gorget around the cheek to behind the eye. There is a band of greenish-bronze across the center of the breast, which merges into a pale gray belly and vent. The short, rounded tail is bronze-green, the central feathers are tipped black, and the three outer feathers are grayish with white tips and a narrow black subterminal band. Females lack the male's violet crown and gorget and have only a brownish-green crown and an off-white chin and throat. Occasionally, there are a few purple markings on the throat. It has a short and straight blackish bill.

Breeding starts as early as February. The nest site can be up to ten feet above the ground in the thick outer foliage of a shrub or tree, but a more open site such as a cactus is occasionally chosen. A cup-shaped nest is constructed from plant fibers and spiderwebs, decorated on the outside with small pieces of lichen, dry leaf, grass, and bark. Plant down and tiny feathers are often used as lining. The female incubates two eggs for a little over two weeks, and the young take about three weeks to fledge.

Calliope Hummingbird

Stellula calliope • 2³/₄–3 inches (7–7¹/₂ cm)

This species is recognized as North America's smallest bird. Many migrate 2,800 miles from their wintering grounds in the southwest part of central Mexico to breed as far north as southwest Canada. Others choose to stop off in the cool montane regions of the Sierra Nevada stretching from Washington to Southern California and also eastward to the Rocky Mountains. Here, they search for suitable breeding territory, areas of new growth after logging or forest fires, where shrubs and low trees proliferate. Their wintering habitat is similar, often associated with shrubby growth following fires, but they are also found in scrub bordering farms and ranches, as well as open pine-oak forests. During the breeding season, they depend on a succession of a wide range of colorful, tube-shaped flowers among which they can forage for nectar. They also hawk among hordes of tiny flying insects. The situation is slightly different in the winter habitat, where competition with other species of hummingbirds and warblers forces them to seek out plant sources in lesser demand.

The male is recognized by his unusual gorget—an array of iridescent purple-magenta elongated feathers that emanates under the chin and spreads outward as radial lines. The upperparts are metallic bronze-green, and the underparts are whitish with a green tinge at the flanks.

The tips of the dark green wing primaries extend past the tip of the tail as the bird is perched. The short tail is greenish-black and the short, straight bill is black. The female is similar to the male but lacks the gorget and has a whitish throat spotted with brown markings. She also has buffish underparts. Her tail feathers are black, and the three outer feathers are tipped with white spots.

Nesting occurs from May to July, when a cup-shaped nest is constructed among foliage, often in a conifer, where it will be protected from adverse weather. Fine plant fibers are held together with spiderwebs and are covered on the outside by a collection of lichens and bits of bark and moss. The inside is lined with plant down. The female incubates her two eggs for just over two weeks, and the young fledge after another three weeks.

Scintillant Hummingbird

Selasphorus scintilla • 2³/₄ inches (7 cm)

Above: A male Scintillant Hummingbird (*Selasphorus scintilla*).

Opposite: A female Scintillant Hummingbird (*Selasphorus scintilla*).

Found only in a confined area of the mountains of Costa Rica and western Panama, and then mainly on the southern slopes, this small hummingbird is more a bird of open countryside. It is found particularly in pastureland scattered with shrubby growth and hedgerows and often approaches human habitation, coming into yards and agricultural land. Shrubby growth within plantations and along forest edges are also exploited. Nectar is taken from a wide variety of small flowers but mainly from low-growing plants and shrubs. Insects and spiders are gleaned from foliage, especially along hedgerows, and hawking for insects is often undertaken from a prominent perch.

The male has bronze-green upperparts, contrasting with a mainly rufous tail. The shafts of the inner tail feathers are bordered with a black longitudinal band, and the outer three tail feathers have a black subterminal band. He has an orange-red gorget with extended feathers at the rear and a small white spot behind the eye. Below the gorget and along the top of the breast is a white band that blends into rufous-buff with greenish markings toward the flanks, leaving a whitish patch down the center of the belly. Both the vent and undertail coverts are a pale rufous color. The short, straight bill is black. The female is similar but is less bright and lacks the red gorget. She has a buff-colored throat spotted with dark gray, which becomes almost black at the ear coverts. Her tail also differs in that it has a broader subterminal black band and a greenish tinge to the inner feathers.

Breeding is confined mainly to the wet season, from September to February, when a suitable site is chosen—usually on an outside branch of a shrub but occasionally among tall grasses. The small, delicate nest is made of fine plant fibers and thistledown with pieces of moss, lichen, and tree fern bound together with spiderwebs and sometimes lined with tiny soft feathers. The outside may be covered with pieces of moss and lichen. Two eggs are usually laid, but no other breeding details are available.

Broad-tailed Hummingbird

Selasphorus platycercus • 4 inches (10 cm)

Above: A female Broad-tailed Hummingbird (*Selasphorus platycercus*).

Opposite: A male Broad-tailed Hummingbird (*Selasphorus platycercus*).

The breeding range of this mainly migrant species covers an area from the highlands of Guatemala northward through the highlands of Mexico and into the United States, where it is spread through southwestern Texas and Arizona and up into eastern California, Nevada, Utah, southern Idaho, and Wyoming. The migrants, mainly from the north of the range, winter in the south from Mexico to Guatemala. It prefers woodland and meadows between 5,000 feet and 8,000 feet, and is often found close to rivers and streams. Its main diet is nectar from flowering ground-hugging shrubs and herbs, but it does glean foliage for spiders and insects, and also hawks flies in the air.

The upperparts of the male are a dark olive-green with a bronze tinge to the central tail feathers. The remaining tail feathers are blackish-purple, tinged red on the outer webs. The gorget is iridescent bright red, below which is a white breast band that stretches in a narrow stripe upward and behind the dark olive ear coverts. The lower breast is whitish, and becomes green at the flanks. His short, straight bill is black. The female is more yellow-green above and has green central tail feathers. The remaining tail feathers are rufous at the base, becoming green toward a black subterminal band, and have a white tip. She has whitish underparts, pale rufous at the flanks and vent, and a spotted rufous-gray throat.

Breeding takes place between April and July, when a small, cup-shaped nest, mainly of very fine plant fibers, is constructed on a branch, frequently overhanging water. Small pieces of lichen, bark, twig, and leaves are used to decorate and disguise the external appearance. The female incubates a clutch of two eggs for two and a half weeks. The chicks take three to four weeks to fledge.

Rufous Hummingbird

Selasphorus rufus • 3¹/₂ inches (8¹/₂ cm)

This migratory species spends its winter mainly in the highlands of Mexico, but it is regularly seen all along the United States' Gulf Coast and in southern Texas. It migrates northward early in the year, arriving in Oregon in late February and spreading farther north as flowering plants become available. Eventually, it spreads throughout its breeding range, which covers the northwestern United States and southwestern Canada as far north as southeastern Alaska and eastward to western Alberta. It obviously prefers cool climates that have a wide variety of flowering plants, but is known to take tree sap from holes made by woodpeckers when flowers are less numerous. Flowering trees are exploited, as are plants such as the opuntias and agaves, and spiders and insects are taken when gleaning through foliage. Within its breeding range, it seems to prefer clearings and forest edges, particularly secondary growth and thorn forests.

As would be expected, the male is of outstanding rufous plumage, in

162

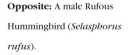

Opposite: A male Rufous Hummingbird (*Selasphorus rufus*).

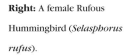

Right: A female Rufous Hummingbird (*Selasphorus rufus*).

165

Above: A male Rufous Hummingbird (*Selasphorus rufus*).

Opposite above: A juvenile Rufous Hummingbird (*Selasphorus rufus*).

Opposite: A female Rufous Hummingbird (*Selasphorus rufus*).

particular its upperparts. The gorget is an iridescent scarlet-red that ranges to bright green as the lighting changes. Below this is a white band on the upper chest that becomes rufous on the belly. The forehead, crown, and a patch at the bend of the wing are bronze-green, and the rounded tail is rufous with a black tip. The female has predominantly bronze-green upperparts down to the central tail feathers. The outer tail feathers are rufous at the base, with green and then black subterminal bands and a white tip. Her underparts are dirty white with a whitish neck and throat. The throat is often covered with iridescent bronze spots.

Nesting sites are variable but are usually on a branch of a shrub or tree. The cup-shaped nest is constructed from mixed plant fibers bound together with spiderwebs and is decorated externally with small pieces of lichen, moss, bark, and leaf. The female incubates two eggs for two and a half weeks, and the young fledge about three weeks later.

Allen's Hummingbird

Selasphorus sasin • 3³/₄ inches (9¹/₂ cm)

Two subspecies of the Allen's Hummingbird exist: the sedentary *S. s. sedentarius* is found on the islands off Southern California, whereas the nominate and migratory subspecies, *S. s. sasin*, winters in southern central Mexico and breeds from Southern California northward to the border of Oregon. Both subspecies seem to favor a more open and scrubby habitat, with a preference for more humid conditions found in canyons and beside streams during the breeding season. After breeding, they disperse and can be found along forest edges and in more open coniferous and deciduous woodland as well as grassland with plenty of shrubby growth. They are nectar feeders with a particular attraction to flowering trees and shrubs, and will also hawk for aerial insects.

As for plumage, this species is frequently confused with the Rufous Hummingbird *(Selasphorus rufus)* where their ranges overlap in Southern California. Males can be distinguished by their iridescent all-green back and nape, which are rufous on the Rufous Hummingbird. However, females and immature birds are virtually indistinguishable. Besides having a green back, the male's forehead and crown are also iridescent green. The rump and upper tail coverts are rufous, leading into tail feathers that are rufous at the base and tipped black. Black edges show on the outer vanes of the outer two tail feathers. The gorget is a brilliant orange-red, below which is a band of white stretching across the breast and narrowing toward the nape. The rest of the underparts are rufous and the shortish black bill is almost straight. There is a small white spot behind the eye and a broad rufous eyestripe passing from the lores above and below the eye, between the crown and gorget, to the nape. Females and immature individuals have predominantly bronze-green upperparts down to and including the central tail feathers. The outer tail feathers are rufous at the base, with green and then black subterminal bands and a

Opposite: A male Allen's Hummingbird (*Selasphorus sasin*).

Below: A female Allen's Hummingbird (*Selasphorus sasin*).

white tip. Her underparts are dirty white and become rufous at the flanks, and she has a whitish neck and throat. The throat is often covered with iridescent bronze spots that become denser over the ear coverts.

The breeding season is throughout the year for the island subspecies (*S. s. sedentarius*), but is confined to spring and early summer for the migrants (*S. s. sasin*). Tree sites are usually chosen for nesting. The nest is built from plant fibers and down, incorporating moss, hair, and lichen, with liberal amounts of spiderwebs to hold it together. The female, who constructs the nest, incubates the eggs alone for two to three weeks. She also feeds the young during the fledging period, which is around three and a half weeks. Two broods are often attempted.

A Checklist of Hummingbirds of the World

Phaethornithinae

Saw-billed Hermit	*Ramphodon naevis*
White-tipped Sicklebill	*Eutoxeres aquila*
Buff-tailed Sicklebill	*Eutoxeres condamini*
Hook-billed Hermit	*Glaucis dohrnii*
Hairy Hermit	*Glaucis hirsuta*
Bronzy Hermit	*Glaucis aenea*
Band-tailed Barbthroat	*Threnetes ruckeri*
Pale-tailed Barbthroat	*Threnetes niger*
Broad-tipped Hermit	*Anopetia gounellei*
White-whiskered Hermit (below)	*Phaethornis yaruqui*
Green Hermit	*Phaethornis guy*
White-bearded Hermit	*Phaethornis hispidus*
Western Long-tailed Hermit	*Phaethornis longirostris*
Eastern Long-tailed Hermit	*Phaethornis superciliosus*
Great-billed Hermit	*Phaethornis malaris*
Tawny-bellied Hermit (opposite)	*Phaethornis syrmatophorus*

Koepcke's Hermit	*Phaethornis koepckeae*
Needle-billed Hermit	*Phaethornis philippii*
Straight-billed Hermit	*Phaethornis bourcieri*
Pale-bellied Hermit	*Phaethornis anthophilus*
Scale-throated Hermit	*Phaethornis eurynome*
Planalto Hermit	*Phaethornis pretrei*
Sooty-capped Hermit	*Phaethornis augusti*
Buff-bellied Hermit	*Phaethornis subochraceus*
Dusky-throated Hermit	*Phaethornis squalidus*
Streak-throated Hermit	*Phaethornis rupurumii*
Little Hermit	*Phaethornis longuemareus*
Minute Hermit	*Phaethornis idaliae*
Cinnamon-throated Hermit	*Phaethornis nattereri*
Reddish Hermit	*Phaethornis ruber*
White-browed Hermit	*Phaethornis stuarti*
Black-throated Hermit	*Phaethornis atrimentalis*
Stripe-throated Hermit	*Phaethornis striigularis*
Gray-chinned Hermit	*Phaethornis griseogularis*

Trochilinae

Tooth-billed Hummingbird	*Androdon aequatorialis*
Green-fronted Lancebill	*Doryfera ludovicae*
Blue-fronted Lancebill	*Doryfera johannae*
Scaly-breasted Hummingbird	*Campylopterus cuvierii*
Wedge-tailed Sabrewing	*Campylopterus curvipennis*
Gray-breasted Sabrewing	*Campylopterus largipennis*
Rufous Sabrewing	*Campylopterus rufus*
Rufous-breasted Sabrewing	*Campylopterus hyperythrus*
Violet Sabrewing	*Campylopterus hemileucurus*
White-tailed Sabrewing	*Campylopterus ensipennis*
Lazuline Sabrewing	*Campylopterus falcatus*
Santa Marta Sabrewing	*Campylopterus phainopeplus*
Napo Sabrewing	*Campylopterus villaviscensio*
Buff-breasted Sabrewing	*Campylopterus duidae*
Sombre Hummingbird	*Campylopterus cirrochloris*
Swallow-tailed Hummingbird	*Campylopterus macrourus*
White-necked Jacobin	*Florisuga mellivora*
Black Jacobin	*Florisuga fusca*
Brown Violet-ear	*Colibri delphinae*
Green Violet-ear	*Colibri thalassinus*
Sparkling Violet-ear	*Colibri coruscans*
White-vented Violet-ear	*Colibri serrirostris*
Green-throated Mango	*Anthracothorax viridigula*
Green-breasted Mango	*Anthracothorax prevostii*
Black-throated Mango	*Anthracothorax nigricollis*
Veragues Mango	*Anthracothorax veraguensis*
Antillean Mango	*Anthracothorax dominicus*
Green Mango	*Anthracothorax viridis*
Jamaican Mango	*Anthracothorax mango*

Fiery-throated Awlbill	*Anthracothorax recurvirostris*
Crimson Topaz	*Topaza pella*
Purple-throated Carib	*Eulampis jugularis*
Green-throated Carib	*Eulampis holosericeus*
Ruby Topaz	*Chrysolampis mosquitus*
Antillean Crested Hummingbird	*Orthorhynchus cristatus*
Violet-headed Hummingbird	*Klais guimeti*
Plovercrest	*Stephanoxis lalandi*
Emerald-chinned Hummingbird	*Abeillia abeillei*
Tufted Coquette	*Lophornis ornatus*
Dot-eared Coquette	*Lophornis gouldii*
Frilled Coquette	*Lophornis magnificus*
Short-crested Coquette	*Lophornis brachylophus*
Rufous-crested Coquette	*Lophornis delattrei*
Spangled Coquette	*Lophornis stictolophus*
Festive Coquette	*Lophornis chalybeus*
Peacock Coquette	*Lophornis pavoninus*
Black-crested Coquette	*Lophornis helenae*
White-crested Coquette	*Lophornis adorabilis*
Wire-crested Thorntail	*Discosura popelairii*
Black-bellied Thorntail	*Discosura langsdorfi*
Coppery Thorntail	*Discosura letitiae*
Green Thorntail (above)	*Discosura conversii*

Racquet-tailed Coquette	*Discosura longicauda*
Red-billed Streamertail	*Trochilus polytmus*
Black-billed Streamertail	*Trochilus scitulus*
Blue-chinned Sapphire	*Chlorostilbon notatus*
Blue-tailed Emerald	*Chlorostilbon mellisugus*
Chiribiquete Emerald	*Chlorostilbon olivaresi*
Glittering-bellied Emerald	*Chlorostilbon aureoventris*
Cuban Emerald	*Chlorostilbon ricordii*
Hispaniolan Emerald	*Chlorostilbon swainsonii*
Puerto Rican Emerald	*Chlorostilbon maugaeus*
Coppery Emerald	*Chlorostilbon russatus*
Narrow-tailed Emerald	*Chlorostilbon stenurus*
Green-tailed Emerald	*Chlorostilbon alice*
Short-tailed Emerald	*Chlorostilbon poortmani*
Fiery-throated Hummingbird	*Panterpe insignis*
White-tailed Emerald	*Elvira chionura*
Coppery-headed Emerald	*Elvira cupreiceps*
Oaxaca Hummingbird	*Eupherusa cyanophrys*
White-tailed Hummingbird	*Eupherusa poliocerca*
Stripe-tailed Hummingbird	*Eupherusa eximia*
Black-bellied Hummingbird (above)	*Eupherusa nigriventris*
Pirre Hummingbird	*Goethalsia bella*
Violet-capped Hummingbird	*Goldmania violiceps*
Dusky Hummingbird	*Cynanthus sordidus*
Broad-billed Hummingbird	*Cynanthus latirostris*
Blue-headed Hummingbird	*Cyanophaia bicolor*
Mexican Woodnymph	*Thalurania ridgwayi*
Purple-crowned Woodnymph	*Thalurania columbica*

Green-crowned Woodnymph	*Thalurania fannyi*
Fork-tailed Woodnymph	*Thalurania furcata*
Long-tailed Woodnymph	*Thalurania watertonii*
Violet-capped Woodnymph	*Thalurania glaucopis*
Violet-bellied Hummingbird	*Damophila julie*
Sapphire-throated Hummingbird	*Lepidopyga coeruleogularis*
Sapphire-bellied Hummingbird	*Lepidopyga lilliae*
Shining Green Hummingbird	*Lepidopyga goudoti*
Blue-throated Goldentail	*Hylocharis eliciae*
Rufous-throated Sapphire	*Hylocharis sapphirina*
White-chinned Sapphire	*Hylocharis cyanus*
Gilded Hummingbird	*Hylocharis chrysura*
Blue-headed Sapphire	*Hylocharis grayi*
Golden-tailed Sapphire	*Chrysuronia oenone*
White-throated Hummingbird	*Leucochloris albicollis*
White-tailed Goldenthroat	*Polytmus guainumbi*
Tepui Goldenthroat	*Polytmus milleri*
Green-tailed Goldenthroat	*Polytmus theresiae*

Buffy Hummingbird	*Leucippus fallax*
Tumbes Hummingbird	*Leucippus baeri*
Spot-throated Hummingbird	*Leucippus taczanowskii*
Olive-spotted Hummingbird	*Leucippus chlorocercus*
White-bellied Hummingbird	*Leucippus chionogaster*
Green-and-white Hummingbird	*Leucippus viridicauda*
Many-spotted Hummingbird	*Leucippus hypostictus*
Rufous-tailed Hummingbird	*Amazilia tzacatl*
Chestnut-bellied Hummingbird	*Amazilia castaneiventris*
Amazalia Hummingbird	*Amazilia amazalia*
Loja Hummingbird	*Amazilia alticola*
Buff-bellied Hummingbird	*Amazilia yucatanensis*
Cinnamon Hummingbird	*Amazilia rutila*
Plain-bellied Emerald	*Agyrtria leucogaster*
Versicolored Emerald	*Agyrtria versicolor*
Blue-green Emerald	*Agyrtria rondoniae*
White-chested Emerald	*Agyrtria brevirostris*
Andean Emerald (previous page)	*Agyrtria franciae*
White-bellied Emerald	*Agyrtria candida*
Azure-crowned Hummingbird	*Agyrtria cyanocephala*
Violet-crowned Hummingbird	*Agyrtria violiceps*
Green-fronted Hummingbird	*Agyrtria viridifrons*
Glittering-throated Emerald	*Polyerata fimbriata*
Sapphire-spangeled Emerald	*Polyerata lactea*
Blue-chested Hummingbird	*Polyerata amabilis*
Purple-chested Hummingbird	*Polyerata rosenbergi*
Mangrove Hummingbird	*Polyerata boucardi*
Honduran Emerald	*Polyerata luciae*
Steely-vented Hummingbird	*Saucerottia saucerrottei*
Indigo-capped Hummingbird	*Saucerottia cyanifrons*
Snowy-breasted Hummingbird	*Saucerottia edward*
Blue-tailed Hummingbird	*Saucerottia cyanura*
Berylline Hummingbird	*Saucerottia beryllina*
Green-bellied Hummingbird	*Saucerottia viridigaster*
Copper-tailed Hummingbird	*Saucerottia cupreicauda*
Copper-rumped Hummingbird	*Saucerottia tobaci*
Snowcap	*Microchera albocoronata*
Blossomcrown	*Anthocephala floriceps*
White-veined Plumeleteer	*Chalybura buffonii*
Bronze-tailed Plumeleteer	*Chalybura urochrysia*
Blue-throated Hummingbird	*Lampornis clemenciae*
Amethyst-throated Hummingbird	*Lampornis amethystinus*
Green-throated Mountain-gem	*Lampornis viridipallens*
Green-breasted Mountain-gem	*Lampornis sybillae*
White-bellied Mountain-gem	*Lampornis hemileucus*
Variable Mountain-gem	*Lampornis castaneoventris*
Xantuss Hummingbird	*Basilinna xantusii*
White-eared Hummingbird	*Basilinna leucotis*
Garnet-throated Hummingbird	*Lamprolaima rhami*
Speckled Hummingbird	*Adelomyia melanogenys*
Ecuadorian Piedtail	*Phlogophilus hemileucurus*
Peruvian Piedtail	*Phlogophilus harterti*

174

Brazilian Ruby	*Clytolaema rubricauda*
Gould's Jewelfront	*Heliodoxa aurescens*
Fawn-breasted Brilliant	*Heliodoxa rubinoides*
Violet-fronted Brilliant	*Heliodoxa leadbeateri*
Velvet-browed Brilliant	*Heliodoxa xanthogonys*
Black-throated Brilliant	*Heliodoxa schreibersii*
Pink-throated Brilliant	*Heliodoxa gularis*
Rufous-webbed Brilliant	*Heliodoxa branickii*
Empress Brilliant (above)	*Heliodoxa imperatrix*
Green-fronted Brilliant	*Heliodoxa jacula*
Magnificent Hummingbird	*Eugenes fulgens*
Scissor-tailed Hummingbird	*Hylonympha macrocerca*
Violet-chested Hummingbird	*Sternclyta cyanopectus*

White-tailed Hillstar	*Urochroa bougueri*
Buff-tailed Coronet (left)	*Boissonneaua flavescens*
Chestnut-breasted Coronet (below)	*Boissonneaua matthewsii*
Velvet-purple Coronet	*Boissonneaua jardini*
Shining Sunbeam	*Aglaeactis cupripennis*
White-tufted Sunbeam	*Aglaeactis castelnaudii*
Purple-backed Sunbeam	*Aglaeactis aliciae*
Black-hooded Sunbeam	*Aglaeactis pamela*
Andean Hillstar	*Oreotrochilus estella*
Ecuadorian Hillstar (following page)	*Oreotrochilus chimborazo*
Green-headed Hillstar	*Oreotrochilus stolzmanni*
White-sided Hillstar	*Oreotrochilus leucopleurus*
Black-breasted Hillstar	*Oreotrochilus melanogaster*
Wedge-tailed Hillstar	*Oreotrochilus adela*
Mountain Velvetbreast	*Lafresnaya lafresnayi*
Bronzy Inca	*Coeligena coeligena*
Brown Inca	*Coeligena wilsoni*
Black Inca	*Coeligena prunellei*
Collared Inca	*Coeligena torquata*
Gould's Inca	*Coeligena inca*
White-tailed Starfrontlet	*Coeligena phalerata*

Golden Starfrontlet	*Coeligena eos*
Golden-bellied Starfrontlet	*Coeligena bonapartei*
Blue-throated Starfrontlet	*Coeligena helianthea*
Buff-winged Starfrontlet	*Coeligena lutetiae*
Violet-throated Starfrontlet	*Coeligena violifer*
Rainbow Starfrontlet	*Coeligena iris*
Sword-billed Hummingbird	*Ensifera ensifera*
Great Sapphirewing	*Pterophanes cyanopterus*
Giant Hummingbird	*Patagona gigas*
Green-backed Firecrown	*Sephanoides sephanoides*
Juan Fernandez Firecrown	*Sephanoides fernandensis*
Orange-throated Sunangel	*Heliangelus mavors*
Longuemare's Sunangel	*Heliangelus clarissae*
Amethyst-throated Sunangel	*Heliangelus amethysticollis*
Gorgeted Sunangel	*Heliangelus strophianus*
Tourmaline Sunangel (opposite)	*Heliangelus exortis*
Little Sunangel	*Heliangelus micraster*
Purple-throated Sunangel	*Heliangelus viola*
Royal Sunangel	*Heliangelus regalis*
Black-breasted Puffleg	*Eriocnemis nigrivestris*
Glowing Puffleg	*Eriocnemis vestitus*
Black-thighed Puffleg	*Eriocnemis derbyi*
Turquoise-throated Puffleg	*Eriocnemis godini*
Coppery-bellied Puffleg	*Eriocnemis cupreoventris*
Sapphire-vented Puffleg (page 180)	*Eriocnemis luciani*
Coppery-naped Puffleg	*Eriocnemis sapphiropygia*
Golden-breasted Puffleg	*Eriocnemis mosquera*
Blue-capped Puffleg	*Eriocnemis glaucopoides*

Colorful Puffleg	*Eriocnemis mirabilis*
Emerald-bellied Puffleg	*Eriocnemis alinae*
Greenish Puffleg	*Haplophaedia aureliae*
Buff-thighed Puffleg	*Haplophaedia assimilis*
Hoary Puffleg	*Haplophaedia lugens*
Purple-bibbed Whitetip (below)	*Urosticte benjamini*
Rufous-vented Whitetip	*Urosticte ruficrissa*
Booted Racquet-tail	*Ocreatus underwoodii*
Black-tailed Trainbearer	*Lesbia victoriae*
Green-tailed Trainbearer	*Lesbia nuna*
Red-tailed Comet	*Sappho sparganura*
Bronze-tailed Comet	*Polyonymus caroli*
Purple-backed Thornbill	*Ramphomicron microrhynchum*
Black-backed Thornbill	*Ramphomicron dorsale*
Bearded Mountaineer	*Oreonympha nobilis*
Bearded Helmetcrest	*Oxypogon guerinii*
Tyrian Metaltail	*Metallura tyrianthina*
Perija Metaltail	*Metallura iracunda*
Scaled Metaltail	*Metallura aeneocauda*
Fire-throated Metaltail	*Metallura eupogon*
Coppery Metaltail	*Metallura theresiae*
Neblina Metaltail	*Metallura odomae*
Violet-throated Metaltail	*Metallura baroni*
Viridian Metaltail	*Metallura williami*
Black Metaltail	*Metallura phoebe*
Rufous-capped Thornbill	*Chalcostigma ruficeps*
Olivaceous Thornbill	*Chalcostigma olivaceum*
Blue-mantled Thornbill	*Chalcostigma stanleyi*
Bronze-tailed Thornbill	*Chalcostigma heteropogon*
Rainbow-bearded Thornbill	*Chalcostigma herrani*
Mountain Avocetbill	*Opisthoprora euryptera*
Gray-bellied Comet	*Taphrolesbia griseiventris*

181

Long-tailed Sylph	*Aglaiocercus kingi*
Violet-tailed Sylph (opposite)	*Aglaiocercus coelestis*
Venezuelan Sylph	*Aglaiocercus berlepschi*
Hyacinth Visorbearer	*Augastes scutatus*
Hooded Visorbearer	*Augastes lumachella*
Wedge-billed Hummingbird	*Augastes geoffroyi*
Purple-crowned Fairy	*Heliothryx barroti*
Black-eared Fairy	*Heliothryx aurita*
Horned Sungem	*Heliactin bilopha*
Marvelous Spatuletail	*Loddigesia mirabilis*
Plain-capped Starthroat	*Heliomaster constantii*
Long-billed Starthroat	*Heliomaster longirostris*
Stripe-breasted Starthroat	*Heliomaster squamosus*
Blue-tufted Starthroat	*Heliomaster furcifer*
Oasis Hummingbird	*Rhodopis vesper*
Peruvian Sheartail	*Thaumastura cora*
Sparkling-tailed Woodstar	*Tilmatura dupontii*
Slender Sheartail	*Doricha enicura*
Mexican Sheartail	*Doricha eliza*
Bahama Woodstar	*Calliphlox evelynae*
Magenta-throated Woodstar	*Calliphlox bryantae*
Purple-throated Woodstar	*Calliphlox mitchellii*
Amethyst Woodstar	*Calliphlox amethystina*
Slender-tailed Woodstar	*Microstilbon burmeisteri*
Lucifer Hummingbird	*Calothorax lucifer*
Beautiful Hummingbird	*Calothorax pulcher*
Vervain Hummingbird	*Mellisuga minima*
Bee Hummingbird	*Mellisuga helenae*
Ruby-throated Hummingbird	*Archilochus colubris*
Black-chinned Hummingbird	*Archilochus alexandri*
Anna's Hummingbird	*Calypte anna*
Costa's Hummingbird	*Calypte costae*
Bumblebee Hummingbird	*Atthis heloisa*
Wine-throated Hummingbird	*Atthis ellioti*
Calliope Hummingbird	*Stellula calliope*
Purple-collared Woodstar	*Myrtis fanny*
Chilean Woodstar	*Myrtis yarrellii*
Short-tailed Woodstar	*Myrmia micrura*
White-bellied Woodstar	*Chaetocercus mulsant*
Little Woodstar	*Chaetocercus bombus*
Gorgeted Woodstar	*Chaetocercus heliodor*
Santa Marta Woodstar	*Chaetocercus astreans*
Esmeraldas Woodstar	*Chaetocercus berlepschi*
Rufous-shafted Woodstar	*Chaetocercus jourdanii*
Volcano Hummingbird	*Selasphorus flammula*
Scintillant Hummingbird	*Selasphorus scintilla*
Glow-throated Hummingbird	*Selasphorus ardens*
Broad-tailed Hummingbird	*Selasphorus platycercus*
Rufous Hummingbird	*Selasphorus rufus*
Allen's Hummingbird	*Selasphorus sasin*

Hummingbird Hot Spots

Arizona
Arizona-Sonora Desert Museum, Tucson
Beatty's Apiary and Orchard, Miller Canyon
Cave Creek Canyon, Portal
Ramsey Canyon Mile Hi Preserve
Santa Rita Lodge, Madera Canyon
Southeastern Arizona Bird Observatory, Bisbee
Wally and Marion Paton's House, Patagonia

Texas
Rockport
Fulton

Trinidad
Asa Wright Nature Center

Costa Rica
Rara Avis Reserve
La Selva Biological Station

Right: A Purple-throated Woodstar (*Calliphlox mitchellii*).

Useful Web Sites

www.birdwatchers.com/debtips.html
Useful feeding and gardening tips to attract hummingbirds.

www.donaldburger.com/bbindex.htm
Donald R. Burger's Web site with details on how to attract hummingbirds in Houston, Texas.

www.flex.net/~lonestar/hummingbird.htm
Hummingbird facts and gardening hints.

www.hummerlady.com
Beth Kingsley Hawkins's picture gallery and notes on hummingbirds.

www.humming-birds.com
Facts and figures about hummingbirds, and gardening and feeding tips for attracting hummingbirds.

www.hummingbirdsociety.org
The official Web site for the Hummingbird Society.

www.hummingbirds.net
Tips on watching, studying, feeding, and gardening to attract North American hummingbirds.

http://ianrnews.unl.edu/static/0603220.shtml
Tips on how to attract hummingbirds to the backyard, hosted by the University of Nebraska-Lincoln, Institute of Agricultural and Natural Resources.

www.nmnh.si.edu/BIRDNET/index.html
The ornithological information resource of the Ornithological Council, hosted by the National Museum of Natural History (Smithsonian Institution).

www.projectwildlife.org/find-hummingbirds.htm
A good resource for dealing with sick and injured hummingbirds.

www.sabo.org/hummers.htm
The official Web site of the Southeastern Arizona Bird Club (SABO),
dedicated to conservation, study, and education for the birds of southeast
Arizona, with a special interest in scientific study and banding of
hummingbirds.

http://hummingbirdworld.com/h
Covers hummingbird behavior, nests, and identification, as well as flowers
that attract hummingbirds.

http://www.wbu.com/edu/hummer.htm
Includes general information as well as answers to questions about feeding,
flight, and other topics.

http://www.hummingbirdforum.com
This helpful forum gives general information on hummingbirds and the
flowers that attract them.

Below: Two Ruby Topazes
(*Chrysolampis mosquitus*)
fight for territory.

Bibliography & Further Reading

Burton, Robert. *The World of the Hummingbird*. Firefly Books, 2001.

Carroll, Don, and Noriko Carroll Andrews. *First Flight: A Mother Hummingbird's Story*. McMeel Publishing, 2006.

del Hoyo, Joseph et al. *Handbook of the Birds of the World, Vol. 5*. Lynx Editions, 1999.

Dennis, John V., and Mathew Tekulsky. *How to Attract Hummingbirds and Butterflies*. Ortho Books, 1991.

Greenewalt, C. H. *Hummingbirds*. Dover Publications Inc., 1991.

Heidcamp, Arnette. *A Hummingbird in My House: The Story of Squeak*. Crown Publishers, 1991.

Howell, Steve. *Hummingbirds of North America: The Photographic Guide*. Princeton University Press, 2003.

Newfield, Nancy L., and Barbara Nielsen. *Hummingbird Gardens*. Houghton Mifflin, 1996.

Roth, Sally. *Attracting Hummingbirds and Butterflies to Your Backyard*. Rodale Books, 2001.

Sargent, Robert. *Ruby-throated Hummingbird Book*. Stackpole Books, 1999.

Schneck, Marcus. *Creating a Hummingbird Garden: A Guide to Identifying Hummingbird Visitors*. Fireside, 1994.

Stokes, Donald, and Lilian Stokes. *Stokes Hummingbird Book*. Little, Brown & Co., 1989.

Toops, Connie. *Hummingbirds: Jewels in Flight*. Voyageur Press, 1992.

Tyrrell, Esther Quesada. *Hummingbirds of the Caribbean*. Crown Publishers, 1990.

Williamson, Sheri. *Attracting and Feeding Hummingbirds*. TFH Publications, 2000.

Williamson, Sheri. *A Field Guide to Hummingbirds of North America (Peterson Field Guides)*. Houghton Mifflin, 2002.

Wyss, Hal H. *Hummingbirds: A Portrait of the Animal World*. Todtri, 1999.

Glossary

Altitudinal migration	Movement from one altitude to another, usually dependent on weather conditions and food availability.
Barbules	The hairy interlocking structures emanating from the feather barbs that form the vane of a feather.
Coracoid	A paired ventral bone of the pectoral girdle.
Coverts	The small feathers at the base of the wings and tail that cover the bases of the larger flight feathers.
Epiphytes	A nonparasitic plant that grows on another plant.
Flight membrane	The main airfoil surfaces formed by the flight feathers on which actual flight depends.
Gorget	A distinctive patch of feathers between the bird's throat and breast.
Gular	The region around the throat.
Hawking	A hovering and chasing habit employed to catch aerial insects.
Iridescent	A shining and colorful appearance of certain feathers due to spectral interference and light scattering, which changes depending on the angle of view.
Lores	The region between the front of the eye and the bill.
Malar	The region on the side of the neck just below the bill and eye.
Melanin	The dark-colored pigments often present in skin and feathers.
Montane	A mountainous region usually above 3,000 feet.
Nape	The region where the back of the neck meets the back of the head.
Nominate	A term applied to the recognized form of a species from which subspecies are thought to have derived.
Platelets	A minute flattened body of cells.
Primary feathers	The flight feathers on the outer joint of the wing corresponding with the human hand.
Primary forest	Original or virgin forest.
Rufous	Reddish-brown color.
Savanna	Open grassland usually scattered with bushes and trees.
Secondary feathers	The flight feathers on the inner wing corresponding with the human forearm.
Secondary forest	New forest growth where original or primary forest has been removed.

189

Left: A Planalto Hermit (*Phaethornis pretrei*).

Index

190

Picture Credits

Page 2: Martin Dollenkamp; page 6: Patricio Herrera; page 7: Juan Bahamón; page 8: Juan Bahamón; page 9: Juan Bahamón; page 10: Academy of Natural Sciences of Philadelphia/Corbis; 11: Steve Byland; page 12: Gianni Dagli Orti/Corbis; page 13: Kevin Schafer/Corbis; page 14: Steve Byland; page 15: Martin Dollenkamp; page 17: Juan Bahamón; page 18: Juan Bahamón; page 19: Juan Bahamón; page 20: Juan Bahamón; page 21: Steve Byland; page 22: Martin Dollenkamp; page 23: Martin Dollenkamp; page 24: Juan Bahamón; page 25: Steve Byland; page 26: Juan Bahamón; page 27: Juan Bahamón; page 28: Kathy Kinnie; page 29 (top): Martin Dollenkamp; page 29 (bottom): Steve Byland; page 30: Juan Bahamón; page 31: Juan Bahamón; page 32: Kathy Kinnie; page 33: Juan Bahamón; page 34: Steve Byland; page 35: Martin Dollenkamp; page 36 (both): Kathy Kinnie; page 37: Kathy Kinnie; page 38: Steve Byland; page 39 (top): Ron Austing/Frank Lane Picture Agency/Corbis; page 39 (bottom): Martin Dollenkamp; page 40 (both): George D. Lepp/Corbis; page 41: George D. Lepp/Corbis; page 42: Martin Dollenkamp; page 44: Martin Dollenkamp; page 45: Juan Bahamón; page 46: Steve Byland; page 47: Juan Bahamón; page 48: Steve Byland; page 49 (both): Steve Byland; page 51: Kevin Schafer/Corbis; page 53: Günter Ziesler; page 55: Juan Bahamón; page 56: Günter Ziesler; page 57: Günter Ziesler; page 58: Kathy Kinnie; page 59: Kathy Kinnie; page 60: Juan Bahamón; page 61: Juan Bahamón; page 62: Kathy Kinnie; page 63: Kathy Kinnie; page 64: Kathy Kinnie; page 65: Juan Bahamón; page 66: Juan Bahamón; page 67: Juan Bahamón; page 69: Kathy Kinnie; page 70: Kathy Kinnie; page 71: Juan Bahamón; page 73: Beth Kingsley Hawkins; page 74: Kathy Kinnie; page 75: Kathy Kinnie; page 76: Wolfgang Kaehler/Corbis; page 77: Luiz Claudio Marigo/Nature Picture Library; page 78: Michael & Patricia Fogden; page 79: Anova Image Library; page 81: Beth Kingsley Hawkins; page 83: Kathy Kinnie; page 84: Kathy Kinnie; page 85: Kathy Kinnie; page 86: Greg W. Lasley; page 87: Greg W. Lasley; page 89: Juan Bahamón; page 90: Kathy Kinnie; page 91: Juan Bahamón; page 93: Michael & Patricia Fogden/Corbis;

page 94: Kathy Kinnie; page 95: Juan Bahamón; page 96: Anova Image Library; page 97: Juan Bahamón; page 98 (both): Kathy Kinnie; page 99: Juan Bahamón; page 101: Günter Ziesler; page 103: Günter Ziesler; page 104: Juan Bahamón; page 105: Juan Bahamón; page 107: Anova Image Library; page 109: Kevin Schafer/Corbis; page 111: Barry Mansell/Nature Picture Library; page 113: Kathy Kinnie; page 114: Juan Bahamón; page 115: Juan Bahamón; page 116: Terry Whittaker/Frank Lane Picture Agency/Corbis; page 117: Tim Zurowski/Corbis; page 118: Kathy Kinnie; page 119: Kathy Kinnie; page 121: Charles Melton/Alamy; page 123: Juan Bahamón; page 124: Kathy Kinnie; page 125: Juan Bahamón; page 126: Juan Bahamón; page 127: Juan Bahamón; page 129: Kathy Kinnie; page 130: Kathy Kinnie; page 131: Juan Bahamón; page 132: Kathy Kinnie; page 133: Juan Bahamón; page 134: Kathy Kinnie; page 135: Kathy Kinnie; page 137: Günter Ziesler; page 138: John Francis/Corbis; page 139: Greg W. Lasley; page 140: Juan Bahamón; page 141: Juan Bahamón; page 143: Günter Ziesler; page 144: Günter Ziesler; page 145: Günter Ziesler; page 147: Juan Bahamón; page 148: Steve Byland; page 149: Juan Bahamón; page 150: Martin Dollenkamp; page 151: Juan Bahamón; page 152: Martin Dollenkamp; page 153: Martin Dollenkamp; page 155: Steve Byland; page 156: Martin Dollenkamp; page 157: Martin Dollenkamp; page 158: Kathy Kinnie; page 159: Juan Bahamón; page 160: Greg Allikas; page 161: Kathy Kinnie; page 162: Martin Dollenkamp; page 163: Martin Dollenkamp; page 164 (both): Martin Dollenkamp; page 165: Martin Dollenkamp; page 166: George Lepp/Corbis; page 167: George Lepp/Corbis; page 168: Juan Bahamón; page 169: Juan Bahamón; page 171: Juan Bahamón; page 172: Juan Bahamón; page 173: Juan Bahamón; page 175: Juan Bahamón; page 176: Juan Bahamón; page 177: Juan Bahamón; page 178: Juan Bahamón; page 179: Juan Bahamón; page 180: Juan Bahamón; page 181: Juan Bahamón; page 183: Juan Bahamón; page 184: Kathy Kinnie; page 186: Kathy Kinnie; page 188: Kathy Kinnie.